PANORAMA OF WORLD ART

———

ART OF
CRETE, MYCENAE, AND GREECE

ART OF
CRETE, MYCENAE,
AND GREECE

Text by GERMAN HAFNER

HARRY N. ABRAMS, INC. Publishers NEW YORK

End papers:

Details from the so-called *Alexander Sarcophagus;* (front) *Alexander in Battle,* (back) *Panther Hunt.*
Marble with rich painting, height of the frieze 27⁵/₈″, over-all length of the sarcophagus 10′5¹/₄″. c. 310 B.C.
From Sidon. Archaeological Museum, Istanbul

Translated from the German by Erika Bizzarri

Library of Congress Catalog Card Number: 68-28392

Contents

Introduction

An awareness of its uniqueness is indispensable to a proper understanding of Greek art. What took place in the art of Greece between the second millennium B.C.—the legendary age of King Minos of Crete and the Homeric heroes—and the time of Alexander the Great and the Diadochi has no counterpart in any other part of the world or in any other age. This is as true of the achievement itself as of the effects that it produced. One must put aside the notion that Greek art merely followed a natural "evolutionary development," as a plant which grows, forms buds, blossoms, and wilts, or as a man who passes from childhood through youth to maturity and old age. While in nature these sequences repeat themselves constantly, each stage inevitably leading to the next, the phenomenon of Greek art was basically different. Nor can one find in the "happy skies" of Greece the reason for the emergence there of the art that was to become the root of all later European art. But as soon as the idea of the history of Greek art as a predestined, inevitable course of events has been shed, then a historical examination of it becomes interesting and exciting, and the great achievements of the Greek artists become individually recognizable. The historical eye can see how these artists reacted to the stimuli of foreign cultures, how they rejected them, cautiously or enthusiastically accepted them, and how they retained what was basically Greek, varied it, and in the end helped it to re-emerge. Times of relative quiet alternated with times of crisis; periods in which art was primarily concerned with problems of form alternated with others in which the depiction of spiritual events predominated. In order to appreciate the decisive turning points in the history of Greek art, the contemporary observer must attempt to transpose himself back to those times and to judge the innovations in the light of their immediate context. The most significant element may otherwise be all too easily overlooked.

THE EARLY PERIOD AND CRETAN-MYCENAEAN CULTURE

The beginnings of Greek art may be traced back to the first appearance of Greek tribes in Hellas. The great conflict between Greek art and that of the East, which was to last for over a thousand years, began here in about 2000 B.C. Pottery finds of the Early and Middle Helladic periods show that the Greek tribes brought with them a geometric, nonrepresentational art, while in the art of the nearby island of Crete and in that of the Orient plants, animals, and human beings were depicted. It is difficult today to re-create the feeling of wonder that must have been aroused in the Greeks, who were accustomed only to monochrome abstract designs, when they first encountered the bright pictorial world which mirrored the colorful life of Crete. This Cretan culture, of which only the legend of Minos, ruler of the seas, of the mysterious Labyrinth, and of the Minotaur which inhabited it was to survive into later ages, is far better known to us in our day, as a result of archaeological excavations, than it was to the Greeks of classical times. It amazes us by the multiplicity of its artistic achievements, by its splendor, by its precise observation of nature, and by the ability of the Cretans to instill into even the humblest object a sense of artistry. There are figures in the round and reliefs, large wall paintings and small pictures painted on vases and engraved in semiprecious stones, yet without any fundamental distinction between the different forms of art. The images could be readily enlarged or reduced and were a free expression of the artists' joy in life, which included the worship of the gods and care for the dead.

6

The Cretan art of the first great palaces greatly fascinated the Greeks, and the transition from the Middle Helladic to the Late Helladic–Mycenaean culture was sudden. The mainland citadels such as Mycenae and Tiryns—later believed to have been built by the Cyclops and to have been the palaces of Agamemnon and other Achaian heroes—were collection centers in which imported Cretan works intermingled with those of immigrant Cretan artists. The native Greek abstract art was almost forgotten. Only in subject matter did the new art of the Greeks differ from the peaceful pictures of Crete, and hunting and battle scenes decorated swords, daggers, and the walls of palaces. With the Mycenaean conquest of Crete, Cretan art was destroyed at its roots and the mainspring of Mycenaean culture was severed. It is also possible that the first rush of enthusiasm for the living art of Crete had already run its course. In any event, a reaction now set in and the old geometric art replaced the art forms of the Cretan world, both in Greece and in Crete. With startling consistency the geometric principle took over and produced a sober and austere geometric art much like the Middle Helladic, with the addition of curvilinear ornamental motifs. The spiral was especially popular in Cycladic art and many Cretan art forms were also based on this lively motif. Whether all this would have lasted cannot be said, for Mycenaean culture came to a violent end. But for all we know, art may already have been started on the road it would assume several centuries later.

GEOMETRIC ART

The immigration of new Greek tribes from the North, classically referred to as the "Doric migrations" and the legendary "Return of the Heraklids," meant little in the field of art, for the art of the newcomers was also geometric. After the destruction of the palaces and the dispersal of the Achaians, social conditions changed into a kind of peasant patriarchy. With the exclusion of the island of Crete, the art of the East became a thing of the past. The provincial crafts, which had survived unscathed, supplied the technical basis for the development of an art which first revealed the Greek artistic drive. Our knowledge of Geometric art depends largely on the rich pottery finds in graves (mostly in the necropolis at the Dipylon gate in Athens). Actually, however, it encompassed all forms of art. The geometric motifs consisting of straight and zigzag lines, triangles, meander bands, circles, and hourglass figures may have had some unknown symbolic meaning to the Greeks. Their precision of execution, apparently rejecting everything that could not be drawn with ruler and compass, reminds us that the Greeks later laid the foundations for the science of geometry. The regular rhythmic recurrence of the motif has often been compared to the hexameter, the poetical meter of the Homeric sagas in the Geometric age. The clarity and precision of ornamentation already seem to point toward that intellectual attitude which was to find its highest expression in the unimpeachable logic of Greek philosophy. The artists of the Geometric period set the formula-like but ever-varying triangle, zigzag, checker, and meander patterns, which symbolized a severe eternal order, in opposition to the unpredictability of nature and the constantly changing ephemeral world around them. By its very nature, Geometric art neither depicts nor narrates: storytelling was for the poets, later thought of as blind and therefore uninfluenced by transitory events and impressions. It is curious that, despite the sharp delineation between the arts, Homeric epic poetry reached its climax at a time when the poets' monopoly of the narrative arts was already beginning to falter. Tales of the pictorial art of the distant East reached Greece; and even though, unlike Mycenaean times, these foreign stimuli were met with great reserve and animal and human figures were accepted only after the corresponding abstract formula had been found, narrative pictures and animal friezes soon found their way into the Geometric potter's stock of ornamental motifs. Battles, chariot rides, scenes of mourning and of lying in state of the dead are among the most common themes. Whether these depict contemporary or heroic events is of no concern here, for they are mere concepts, like the very words "battle" and "mourning," and so may be used indiscriminately. Even where heroes are shown, such "type pictures" still require an identifying inscription. The superiority felt by the poet when faced by these first attempts at pictorial narrative is shown by the manner in which Homer describes the shield of Achilles which, with its rich figural decoration, was made by the god Hephaistos. The poet's advantage, in this respect, over the contemporary Geometric pictorial artist, with the limitations of his craft, is evident to anyone who can share the hero's thoughts as well as hear the description of the broad landscapes and of the ceaselessly moving, dancing, and merrily singing figures that inhabit them.

THE SEVENTH CENTURY B.C.

As colonies were founded and rulers from the East began to leave offerings in Greek temple sanctuaries, the artist's growing familiarity with Eastern works of art increased his awareness of this limitation. However, the high degree of self-awareness that he had attained in the Geometric age offset the danger of a complete capitulation to foreign influences; he could therefore choose at will what he preferred most in Oriental art and so set his own course. The fantastic Oriental creatures which now frequently appeared on pottery were a sign that Greek art was absorbing outside influences. Stylistically this is not so evident, for there is no known case of direct imitation of an Eastern original, and all innovations seemed—and in fact were—Greek. The monumental sculpture which appeared in the seventh century would never have materialized without this stimulus from the East. The awesome effect that such sculpture had on a people accustomed only to small Geometric figures which could be held in the hand could well explain how legends arose telling of how the statues of Daidalos moved of their own accord.

The classic Greek temple also came into being at this time, as well as the long series of animated scenes from Greek legend, which, however, were often provided with explanatory inscriptions, in spite of the much greater clarity of expression now available to the artist. Thus it was that this period was of great importance for the future development of Greek art, confirming as it did both the conscious independence of its aims and its ability to learn from foreign influences. Large-scale sculpture paved the way for the separation of art into categories, for large sculpture and small, as well as painting, each had its own subject matter and purpose.

THE SIXTH CENTURY B.C.

Until the beginning of the Persian Wars, Archaic art unfolded rather leisurely, particularly in the cultural centers which sprang up around the splendid courts of the rulers, or tyrants. The arts stuck to familiar paths and were limited to given types. The profile presentation of the figure was accepted in relief as well as in painting and the artist turned his talents to a refinement of details. The technical perfection of marble sculpture enlivened by painting, the outlines of vase paintings scratched with a graver's needle, and the colorful working of these vases with red and white body colors lend a cheerful air to this apparently self-assured art. The marble statues of confident youths and traditionally garbed maidens have the same air. Archaic art is best embodied in these two types of freestanding sculpture. Pictorial narrative took over in the field of vase painting, and turned vases into veritable picture books of Greek legend as well as providing themes for reliefs and architectonic sculpture.

Both politically and artistically Greece was an aggregate of independent units. Local distinctions are easily recognizable both in the technique and style of the vast quantities of painted ware that have survived; less so in sculpture, where the only guidance is style. Perhaps the rivalry between separate local groups led to the fact that the first signatures of potters and vase painters appeared now. The artists themselves step more into the foreground, and this pride in their craft led them to see in Daidalos their mythical ancestor. The names of individual sculptors are known to us through their signatures or through reference to them in later literature, and it is clear that they, as well as numerous vase painters, had their own individual style.

Archaic Greek art now stood on an even footing with the archaic art of Egypt, Mesopotamia, and Asia Minor. Here, as there, the basic laws of art could be learned and applied. But only in Greece can a restrained urge for expression be sensed, an indication that Greek art alone still had something to offer. The philosophers were no longer satisfied with the "rules of life," and the artists, too, felt the prescribed rules to be unbearable shackles.

THE FIFTH CENTURY B.C.

The downfall of the tyrants and the Persian Wars are symbols and consequences of an intellectual change in Greece, in which the Archaic world was shattered and Greece was liberated from the art and culture of the East. The fifth century was the point of no return between the future and the past. With the destruction of the Acropolis by the Persians, the Archaic figures of maidens were reduced to rubble. Upon this there soon rose the glorious structures of the Parthenon, the Erechtheion, and the Propylaia. The sculptors freed their art from its shackles and breathed new life into it. The invention of hollow bronze casting permitted the creation of large figures in every possible pose, in the same way as small sculpture and painting. Myron's statue of the runner Ladas seemed really about to run off its base. Heroic sculpture in the European sense was produced and small-scale sculpture was judged by comparison with it. The beginnings of large-scale painting by Kimon and Polygnotos belong to this same period, but their works are only known to us through later descriptions. Not only did indications of landscape provide a broader setting, but foreshortened and overlapping figures moved freely within this landscape. Sporadic attempts made by vase painters to draw such figures in rear or angled views suggest the tremendous effects produced by this form of painting and reveal the unbridgeable gap between large-scale painting and vase painting. Later writers stressed the spiritual expression of the figures and the high "ethos" of the painting of Polygnotos, evidence of a fundamentally new trend in opposition to Archaic art. It is significant that these innovations in Greek art—both in form and content—were the work of that generation of artists that lived at the time of the Persian Wars.

The following generation, grouped around Pheidias (who was a friend of the statesman Perikles), created the splendid structures on the Acropolis. The picture thus presented around the middle of the fifth century, later to become known as the "classic" age, was less complicated and calmer. Athens was its center and the Parthenon, with Pheidias' gold and ivory cult statue of Athena, was its symbol. Here the artists met in friendly competition and (as recounted of Pheidias, Polykleitos, Kresilas, and Phradmon) engaged in outright contests with each other and wrote theoretical treatises on their art. This blessed era of peace under such a statesman as Perikles, among whose friends were numbered the great intellects of the time, was unique and was recognized as such. The death of Perikles and the decline of Athens during the Peloponnesian War shattered this harmony. Art now differed from reality in that it was a world of beauty in which the individual as such was his own justification. Sokrates and Euripides emphasized self-responsibility and the psychological problems of man. Paintings by Zeuxis and Parrhasios, and also funerary reliefs, were invitations to reflect on virtue and happiness and on the fate of man, who was responsible for his own destiny. Only large-scale art had the means to express these problems; vase painting had now become a "miniature art."

THE FOURTH CENTURY B.C.

The period leading up to the appearance of Alexander the Great was a time of Greek civil strife. Despite this, philosophy still flourished, based on that of Plato. The visual arts lost their precise contours, and the world of man—recognized as illusionary—was reproduced in translucent marble and in paint as the reflection of an underlying perfect world of divine concepts. The state was considered a subject for philosophic utopias, hardly, however, a matter of real interest otherwise; art therefore turned to the more restricted sphere of the family, the private world of woman and child. The true nature of woman was finally discovered and sculptors and painters never tired of creating variations on the theme of Aphrodite. The childlike *Aphrodite* of Praxiteles was one of the most highly esteemed works of art and, for the first time, showed the goddess totally nude. Praxiteles preferred to work in marble, whose crystalline structure partly absorbed, partly reflected, the light. This created nuances of color and an indistinctness of form that endowed the object with a peculiar radiance. The male figure also became more feminine and less athletic and often seemed lost in a moody dreaminess. Eros and Pothos have their hair arranged in female fashion. Skopas made two statues of the latter—the personification of desire—and other figures by the same Parian master are endued with a similar feeling of pathos. Clearly it was painting that best succeeded in expressing the ideals of the century, and painters such as Nikias, who worked together with Praxiteles, made this the classic age of painting. Nikias transferred mythological events into the realm of personal tragedy. Celebrated in his lifetime, he was honored later with a state funeral. Sculptors and painters required a sympathetic public that would immerse itself in, and surrender itself to, their works.

THE TIME OF ALEXANDER THE GREAT AND THE DIADOCHI

The political changes wrought by Alexander caused Greece to emerge as part of a world empire and put an end to the romantic search for a higher and more beautiful truth. Raw reality again came into its own. Lysippos claimed that the visible reality of man should be shown, and proudly rejected the traditions of the past. His *Apoxyomenos* illustrates this. The space enclosed and dominated by the great sweep of the athlete's body seems to make clear that the restrictiveness of the old spatial relationships has finally been overcome. Leochares, the great sculptor of gods, was also active at the Macedonian court of Alexander. His *Apollo* re-established the boundaries between the divine and the human, which had almost disappeared in the childlike god of Praxiteles. Even so, Apelles painted Alexander with a thunderbolt in his hand. All great men—artists, philosophers, poets, and the cultured public in general—felt a greater kinship with the divine, a tendency that was both gratifying and dangerous. Such men therefore looked all the more lovingly upon the lower orders of the world: peasants, shepherds, and innocent children. Only an educated man could fully understand these works of art with their hidden allusions, references, and allegorical content. Confronted by such works, the ordinary man and the barbarian were merely struck by the display of splendor which glorified not only the princely courts but also the culture of Greece. The indebtedness of art to the achievements of the past was recognized: ancient sculptures and paintings were collected in museums, and the works of writers and poets in great libraries.

In Alexander's time, Greek art was far removed from its origins. This was true not only in a geographical sense (Athens being no longer the sole center, but only one among many including Pella, Pergamon, Antioch, and Alexandria), but much more in the fact that art now placed itself in the service of a ruling elite. The nucleus of this new upper class had its origins in Macedonia, which until then had only participated at the fringe of

Greek culture. The wonderful altar of Pergamon illustrates the degree to which the rulers identified themselves with ancient Greece. Its frieze of the battle between the gods and the giants reflected the victory of Pergamon over the Gauls and also glorified the victory of culture over nonculture. Anyone accepting Greek culture, regardless of his race, had the right to consider himself Greek. King Eumenes II, the builder of the altar, was a faithful ally of Rome and owed to her the extent of his kingdom. The Romans, who had been in contact with Greek culture via Etruria since ancient times, and later more directly through the Greek colonies in southern Italy, soon became the true rulers. As the resistance of the Greek princes to the successful warfare and clever diplomacy of the Romans collapsed, the center of artistic, as well as political, action moved to Rome. The enthusiasm with which the Romans accepted Greek culture may have facilitated once more the reorientation of Greek art. Within the framework of the Roman state and the fundamentally different Roman way of thinking, Greek art met fresh challenges with renewed strength. Greece and the Greek East had become peripheral areas as early as the second century B.C., and the art of these regions has a provincial character. This turn of affairs is revealed in the works of later Roman writers on art, who claimed that Greek art had come to an end with the generation of artists succeeding Lysippos and was not resurrected until the middle of the second century B.C. This new life flourished under the auspices of Rome.

THE TRANSMISSION OF GREEK ART

Any attempt at reconstructing the history of Greek art must take into account the fragmentary state of our knowledge in this field. Every sizable object of gold or silver has been destroyed, and works in bronze, the favorite material of the Greek sculptor, were also liable to be melted down because of the intrinsic value of the metal. Even marble statues were often broken up and burned in the lime kilns. Large paintings have entirely disappeared on account of the ephemeral nature of the walls and panels on which they were painted. As religious ideas changed, whole classes of cult images were destroyed. These included some of the most magnificent works of Greek art, overpowering in their size and in the effect produced by the gold and ivory of which they were made. The forces of nature, temple-shattering earthquakes, the effects of weathering, which deformed the surfaces of bronze and marble sculpture, vandalism, and the ravages of war did the rest. Countless works of art went to the bottom of the seas when the ships which were to transport them from Greece to Rome, or from Rome to Constantinople, sank. The break with tradition at the end of classical times and the loss of interest in pagan works of art throughout the centuries would have resulted in still greater gaps, had not the Romans shown such a lively interest in Greek art. Accounts of Greek artists, data concerning their lives and works, anecdotes, epigrams, extracts of Greek art literature, and the first attempts at a Greek history of art have survived through the ages. The *Natural History* of Pliny (A.D. 23–79) is our main source, although the author was more interested in the marble and bronze and in the pigments used than in the works of art themselves. The Greek travelogues of Pausanias (second century A.D.) supplement Pliny and address themselves to the cultured Roman traveler. They give some idea of the plethora of works of art still extant in the Greece of his time, and the detailed descriptions of some of the masterpieces of Polygnotos and other painters are of inestimable value. Indeed, the more or less accurate accounts of writers are our most important source of knowledge of contemporary painting. Only the older vases can give us some notion of painting of the time, for the paths of this decorative art and of large-scale works on walls and panels diverged in the fifth century B.C. Later vase paintings are only distantly related to the realistic paintings of a Zeuxis or a Parrhasios. The interest which the Romans showed in the Greek art of the past also led to the making of copies. Greek masterpieces were reproduced in bronze and marble and such replicas stood in gardens, halls, libraries, and theaters almost everywhere that was touched by Roman culture. Although most of these copies have been destroyed, especially those in bronze, some have survived; and even though they are only copies, they provide us with a good idea of the original Greek masterpieces. The wall paintings of Pompeii, Herculaneum, and Stabiae, which were buried and preserved by the eruption of Vesuvius in A.D. 79, are probably (in the case of those whose themes coincide with Pliny's lists of paintings by Nikias) copies of famous "classic" Greek works. However, allowance must be made for changes in taste, deliberate "corrections," and concern for the decorative relationship, as well as for the artistic ability of the provincial painters. Copies of Greek statues appear to be more reliable, for any alteration in the composition would have resulted in basic changes. Casts and bronze copies provide the best medium of transmission, but the numerous surviving marble copies were often accurately made to scale by mechanical means. When a different material from that of the original was used, disturbing features such as supports and struts were sometimes necessary. In special cases, the technical difficulties were so great that reproduction in marble was quite out of the question. Such was the case with Myron's famous statue of the runner Ladas; and consequently we have no way of forming a real idea of what this—and many other works—were like. The more copies of a masterpiece that are preserved, the more complete is our knowledge and the better informed can be our judgment. Every replica, however, even small reproductions such as statuettes, reliefs, or engravings on coins or gems, is a welcome aid in our attempt to fill these gaps in our knowledge.

The love that the Romans had for Greek art thus led to its preservation and recognition. Archaic Greek art, even when this had not been long since buried, was ignored, since it did not appeal to Roman taste. As a result, our knowledge of Archaic art depends entirely on what archaeological excavations have brought to light since the freeing of Greece from Turkish domination. Many originals also survived when the Romans thought them too unimportant or when transportation appeared unprofitable and the objects were left on their original sites. Examples include tomb reliefs of the fifth and fourth centuries B.C., statuettes, terra cottas, and the sculptural decoration of temples—carved pediments, friezes, and metopes—preserved with the temples or beneath their ruins. The still older geometric Greek art of the second millennium B.C. was unknown to later Antiquity, or was at best a mere memory of something mythical and unreal. Excavations have revealed a lost world, in the exploration of which archaeology stands entirely on its own. By observing the first steps taken by Greek art right in this earliest period, the subsequent steps become more comprehensible and its historical course can be seen as a constant struggle with problems arising partly from without and partly from within the nature of the Greeks. However, one must continually bear in mind the fragmentary preservation of Greek art. Much upon which its fame was once based has been irretrievably lost. Antiquity evidently considered much of what has survived as unworthy of comment. Nevertheless, what these works reveal about the Greek spirit is still enough to fill us with wonder and admiration.

EARLY PERIOD (Early Helladic, 2500–1900 B.C. Middle Helladic, 1900–1580 B.C.)

The first manifestations of Greek art were extremely modest, yet of an unmistakable and compelling nature: geometric ornamental motifs. Upon their arrival, the immigrating Greeks encountered the unornamented vessels of a culture that dominated the Greek mainland and the coast of Asia Minor. Alien to them, it could exert no stimulus. However, the Cycladic culture (see pages 15, 16) thriving on the islands seemed closer to that of the Greeks on account of its rich ornamentation, and many a stimulus originated there. The fascinating art of Crete began then to exert an overwhelming and ever-increasing influence on the art of the Greeks.

"Sauceboat." Terra cotta with glaze paint, length 10⁷/₈". Early Helladic, 2500–1900 B.C. From Spedos (Naxos). National Museum, Athens

Judging from its shape, this vessel is a typical product of an old pre-Greek culture, but it displays such Greek characteristics in its ornamentation that, both here and in similar vases, the first appearance of the Greeks coming in from the North can be recognized. The latticework triangles, which are also painted on the inner rim of the vessel, belong to the stock of Greek geometric ornamental motifs which was to reach its fullest development a thousand years later (see pages 61–65). This triangle motif, unknown until now in the Greek world, was applied with glaze paint, which, increasingly refined, was to remain the characteristic of Greek vase painting.

13

Kantharos. Terra cotta, height 5¹/₈″. Middle Helladic, 1900–1580 B.C. From Lerna (Argolis). Museum, Argos

The kantharos, a drinking vessel with two high handles protruding above the rim, was passed from hand to hand at banquets. This form appeared here for the first time, and remained a favorite in later ages.

The motifs applied with mat colors articulate the vessel according to its structural form. This reveals the characteristic Greek attitude to the relationship between vessel and ornamentation; both elements must have a vivid relationship to each other and form a unit.

Female Idol. Marble, height c. 4³/₄″. Early Cycladic culture, 2300–2000 B.C. Württembergisches Landesmuseum, Stuttgart

These oldest marble sculptures of the Greek world, the "island idols," have a doll-like character. They are not statuettes because they cannot be stood upright, but were laid as tomb furnishings beside the dead. The flattened shape of the female figure and the schematic representation of details, the nudity and the arms crossed in front of the body characterize most of these figurines. Their real significance is still not clear: they have been interpreted as nymphs, heroized dead, and goddesses.

Pan-shaped vessel (the short handle is missing). Terra cotta, diameter 8⁵/₈". Cycladic, c. 2000 B.C. From Naxos. National Museum, Athens

In addition to the Cycladic idols (see page 15), the old culture on the Greek Cyclades produced a pottery with rich ornamentation, in which curved lines, mainly spirals, predominate.

A "sun" surrounded by a quadruple spiral motif and four fishes are incised on the underside of this vessel, which is flat and has a low steep rim. The use to which these pans were put is unknown; they may have been filled with water and used as mirrors. The play of the curvilinear ornamental motifs, also used to symbolize water, was originally foreign to the Greeks, but apparently the idea soon appealed to them. Numerous works of Mycenaean art (see pages 42, 46–48) testify to the fertilization of Greek art by the Cycladic culture.

CRETAN-MYCENAEAN ART (2800–1100 B.C.)

Cretan-Mycenaean art encompasses two basically different modes of artistic expression which, nonetheless, interpenetrate and overlap in a distinctive way. The art of Crete, which goes back to the third millennium B.C., reached its apogee in the first half of the second millennium. It was characterized by its representational use of human beings, animals, plants, and architecture. By contrast, the Greeks who ruled on the mainland (the citadel of Mycenae gives this culture its name) possessed a geometric decorative art. The encounter between these two extremes, accompanied by the spread of Greek power even on Crete, led to the absolute victory of nonrepresentational art.

How alien the Minoan culture of Crete must have been to the Greeks can be surmised from a comparison of the geometric motifs on their vessels (see pages 13, 14) with the freely moving human form on this sherd. The outline has been sketched with great verve so as to capture the momentary impression of the subject. The dancers, originally probably four, belong to the earliest depictions of human beings in Minoan painting. They were arranged lengthwise to fit the circular form of the foot of the vessel. This, too, completely contradicts Greek feeling.

Dancing Woman, painted in white on the fragmentary foot of a large fruit dish. Terra cotta, height of the figure 4″. Middle Minoan II, 1850–1700 B.C. From Phaistos. Archaeological Museum, Herakleion

Soldier with a Dagger. Terra-cotta statuette, height 6⁷/₈″. Middle Minoan, 2000–1850 B.C. From the sanctuary of Mount Petsofa (on the eastern coast of Crete). Archaeological Museum, Herakleion

This early Minoan sculpture is modeled out of clay as an image of life. It is concerned only with grasping the outer appearance and lacks that penetration into the inner framework, the structure of the human figure, which is so essential to Greek feeling. Unlike the Cycladic idol (page 15), this figure stands unsupported on a small pedestal. The naked man, clad only in a narrow loincloth, holds his hands in front of his breast in the prescribed manner. He is armed only with a dagger and is probably a member of the palace guard. The warrior as subject matter is obviously alien to Minoan culture, which was of a peaceful nature and went without fear of the island being attacked.

Cup in the Kamares style with white and red color on a
brownish-black ground. Terra cotta, height 3″. c. 1800
B.C. From Knossos. Archaeological Museum, Herakleion

Minoan art displays its tremendously imaginative creative power most visibly in the decoration of vessels.
Spiral, round, or bubble-shaped motifs are painted on the ground in bright colors. A particularly fine achievement in the field of ceramics is the so-called eggshellware, which has extremely thin walls. The decoration
of this cup, a large ellipse pointed at both ends enclosing a rosette motif reserved in the ground color, extends
horizontally across the vessel, making it appear soft and alive. To the Greek eye, there is a lack of all precision in the form and decoration of the vessel, as well as in their structural relationship.

Like every Cretan palace, Phaistos at first sight presents a rather bewildering picture: a multiplicity of rooms of various sizes, apparently arranged in a "labyrinthine" manner. The nucleus is a large court, around which are grouped the halls, rooms, and chambers. This centrifugal composition is made possible by the fact that no surrounding wall of any kind determines an exterior boundary. Such arrangements, with a total absence of defensive structures, are conceivable only when neither enemies within nor without need be considered. Here the difference between the Cretan and Mycenaean worlds (see pages 37–39) is most evident. Domination of the seas by Cretan ships apparently guaranteed peace.

Palace of Phaistos (southern Crete). View from the northwest onto the western court of the first palace (2000–1700 B.C.), right foreground; the west wing of the second palace (1700–1400 B.C.) behind. In the background, the plain of Mesara and the Kophinos Mountains

The Cretan relationship to the Orient is indicated by the numerous works of Egyptian faïence—brightly painted reliefs with scenes of the animal world, and colorful statuettes. The best-known probably represents a priestess rather than a goddess. She holds snakes as symbols of the goddess in her hands, and also wears the divine attribute of the lion on her head. The blouse open at the breasts and the long flounced skirt correspond to the court attire of the nobility.

So-called *Snake Goddess*. Brightly painted faïence, height 11⅝″. Middle Minoan, seventeenth century B.C. From the temple depository of Knossos. Archaeological Museum, Herakleion

Like the "*Snake Goddess*" (see page 21), this prince also gives the Minoan world a strange, legendary appearance, combining extreme sophistication with a natural unconcern. The young man wears a distinctive crown consisting of a headband decorated with lily blossoms and three long feathers emerging from a lily. We can only speculate as to the painting of the background. The combination of relief and painting indicates the carefree nature of the Minoan artist.

Prince with the Feather Crown. Relief fresco (greatly restored), height c. 87″. Sixteenth century B.C. From the large vestibule of the west wing of the palace of Knossos. Archaeological Museum, Herakleion

The goblet, opposite, is cut out of soft stone and is ornamented with figures in relief whose posture is adapted to the funnel form of the vessel. The relief figures may be interpreted as an officer of the watch presenting three men (who

Goblet. Steatite, height $4^7/_8''$.
Sixteenth century B.C. From Hagia Triada. Archaeological Museum, Herakleion

carry large shields and who may have come from afar as ambassadors to Crete) to the prince standing in front
of the palace door. But the scene has also been interpreted as a game played by children, imitating events in
the lives of grown-ups.

The pictorial art of Crete could accordingly represent unique or typical events of life and use these as
decoration for vessels. It reflected these events, as in a mirror, no differently from the other visible objects of
the environment and of nature.

Lilies. Fresco, white and green on a dark-red ground, height c. 71″. c. 1600 B.C. From a villa at Amnisos (on the coast near Knossos). Archaeological Museum, Herakleion

The natural world of animals and plants, with its pleasing but at times bizarre forms, repeatedly served Cretan art as inspiration for the loveliest of pictures, revealing an intimate relationship with the surrounding world such as the Greeks were hardly aware of. On a wall of the villa at Amnisos, the blooms of three white lilies growing out of a green cluster of leaves fill a dark-red, stepped depression in a band of light-green stripes, the white color being inlaid into the ground. A certain regularity in the growth of the lily harmonizes with the courtly manner of life of the inhabitants of the palaces and noble villas.

Ornamental frieze of rosettes and columns. Fresco fragment, white, blue, black, red, and brown, height 9½″. Sixteenth century B.C. From the northwest hall of the palace of Knossos. Archaeological Museum, Herakleion

This fragmentary fresco shows, above the frieze of large rosettes, a row of typical Minoan columns, tapering downward, with small double axes in the wide capital area. Between the columns are horned cult symbols. This fragment, probably part of a larger ensemble, provides an idea of Cretan architecture and testifies to the strong religious influences on building. The horns of consecration, known from numerous other Cretan depictions, are an expression of the cult of the bull, echoed in Greek mythology in the figure of the Minotaur (see pages 111, 194), the story of Pasiphaë, the Rape of Europa, and the "Cretan bull."

A light-skinned man, carrying two spears, leads a row of Negroes who follow him at a run. He wears the usual apron, but is distinguished by a close-fitting head covering from which two feathers or horns project. This astonishingly lively figure was part of a larger ensemble depicting some unidentified event. The presence of a Negro guard at the court of a Cretan prince is not surprising, for this culture was, in a sense, an outpost of the Oriental world.

Running Officer. Fresco, height of figure originally c. 6″. Late sixteenth century B.C. From Knossos. Archaeological Museum, Herakleion

Worshiper. Bronze votive figurine, height 6¹/₂″. Late Minoan, c. 1550 B.C. From Tylissos (central Crete). Archaeological Museum, Herakleion

The posture of this man, his left arm hanging down beside his body while his right hand is raised to his forehead, seems to be that of an orant. The statuette is thus a votive figurine, in which prayer becomes an eternal expression of worship. The artist concentrated on the gesture of prayer and on the posture of the man, who is dressed only in a short apron. The strongly concave small of the back and the knees pressed backward correspond to the customary Minoan ideal.

27

Tablet with Linear B script. Clay, height 5⁷/₈″. c. 1550 B.C. From Knossos. Archaeological Museum, Herakleion

The symbols of this syllabic script developed from an older form, Linear A, which has not yet been deciphered, the language in which it is written still being unknown. The more recent script resulted from the adaptation of Linear A to the exigencies of the Greek language. The decipherment of the Linear B tablets, which is still in progress, has identified the language as an early form of Greek. The tablets contain accounts and imply the existence in the palaces, by then in Greek hands, of a surprisingly detailed system of bookkeeping.

Papyrus Stalks, detail of an amphora in the Palace style. Terra cotta, over-all height c. 38″. Fifteenth century B.C. From a house near Knossos. Archaeological Museum, Herakleion

The world of animals and plants, which appears on the walls of villas and palaces (see page 24) in the form of independent pictures or as part of the total decoration, also served as an inexhaustible source of motifs for vase painters.

The papyrus plants which blend ornamentally with the body of the calyx-shaped amphora are partially in relief, partially painted. They grow from a cluster of leaves and frame circle motifs with their blossoms.

Cult vessel in the form of a bull. Terra cotta, length 10″, height 7⅞″. Late Minoan, c. 1500 B.C. From Pseira (Mirabello Bay). Archaeological Museum, Herakleion

This carefully modeled bull has small openings at the nape of the neck and at the nostrils. Such vessels in animal form are very common in Cretan and Mycenaean art (see page 41): in the cult, they probably served for the pouring out of the sacrificial libation. The bull, later to become the emblem of Crete, was central to the religious cults of the Minoan world and commonly appears in paintings and as a symbol (see page 25). Dangerous athletic bull-games were organized in honor of the deity.

Head of a Woman (damaged). Terra
cotta, height 3½″. Late Minoan,
1400–1100 B.C. From the Cave of
Psychro (Lasithi Mountains). Archaeological Museum, Herakleion

That curious mixture of naïveté and elegance characteristic of Minoan femininity, which is evident in some
of the murals, is also a feature of this small head. Naturalness is just as self-evident as the adherence to the
laws of court etiquette. The immediacy of its lively expression is particularly striking in this little head with
its painted lips, eyebrows, lashes, and pupils.

Pair of cups decorated in repoussé with wild and tame bulls. Gold, height 3^1/$_4$″ and 3″. c. 1500 B.C. From a tholos tomb at Vaphio, near Sparta. National Museum, Athens

On one cup (top), a bull is seen running down two men, while others (on the reverse side) are shown entangled in a net and escaping in flight. On the other cup, a cow and a bull stand peacefully side by side in the center, while on one side a herdsman is tethering a captured bull by its hind leg, and on the other a third bull approaches cautiously. These gold reliefs reveal a Minoan style and the choice of theme is also Cretan. They

Detail of the lower cup on the facing page

would thus appear to be imported works of art or, more probably, to have been made by a Cretan artist working on the mainland. Such costly cups throw a revealing light on the way of life of the Greek princes, which differed from conditions in the Early and Middle Helladic periods primarily in its enormous wealth (see pages 13, 14).

Seals with battle and hunting scenes. Gold, lengths $1^3/_8''$ (top), $^3/_4''$ (middle), and $1^1/_8''$ (bottom). Sixteenth century B.C. The oval seals are from shaft grave IV, the rectangular from shaft grave III, of Grave Circle A at Mycenae. National Museum, Athens

Although the style of these deeply engraved seals is Cretan, the choice of subject is Greek-Mycenaean. They are therefore probably the works of Cretans who emigrated to Mycenae. The battle scene is reminiscent of the battles around Troy, while the fight with the lion recalls the story of Herakles and the Nemean lion.

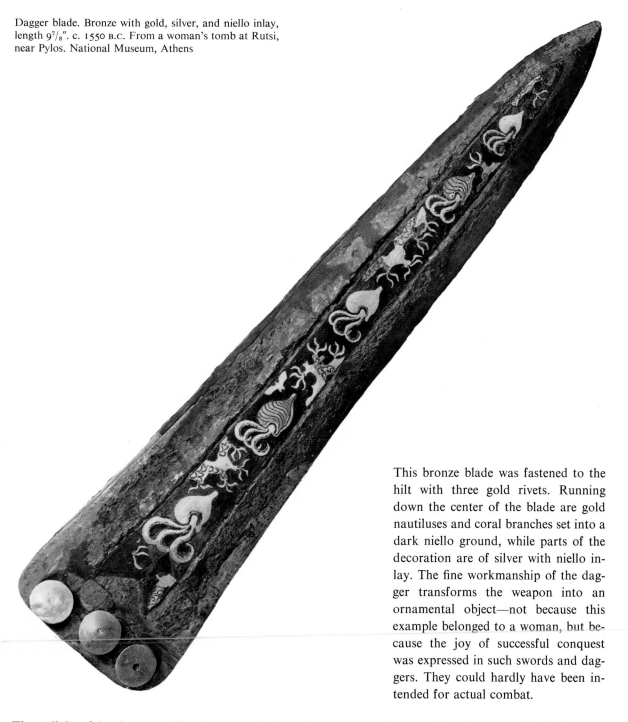

Dagger blade. Bronze with gold, silver, and niello inlay, length 9⁷/₈″. c. 1550 B.C. From a woman's tomb at Rutsi, near Pylos. National Museum, Athens

This bronze blade was fastened to the hilt with three gold rivets. Running down the center of the blade are gold nautiluses and coral branches set into a dark niello ground, while parts of the decoration are of silver with niello inlay. The fine workmanship of the dagger transforms the weapon into an ornamental object—not because this example belonged to a woman, but because the joy of successful conquest was expressed in such swords and daggers. They could hardly have been intended for actual combat.

The delight of battle and of the chase stands in stark contrast to the peaceful enjoyment of life in Crete. It recurs again and again throughout the course of Greek art (see page 233) and even here emerges as a typically Greek characteristic.

Two Women and a Child. Ivory, height 2³/₄″. Fifteenth century B.C. From Mycenae. National Museum, Athens

Two squatting women, dressed in Cretan style, watch over a child playing between them. The women are joined by their arms, which rest upon each other's shoulders, and by a kind of shawl, which they share draped over their backs. It has not yet been possible to identify the group (Cretan in style), but it can be assumed that it expresses a Greek concept, even though nothing similar appears to have been found in later Greek mythology. The adoption of Cretan fashions by the Mycenaean women is of interest.

The Lion Gate, Mycenae. Width of entrance, 9′ 10″; height of sculpture, 9′ 10″. Early thirteenth century B.C.

The fortification walls of Mycenae were of cyclopean construction (using great boulders) except for those parts adjacent to the Lion Gate, which were of ashlar (squared stone). The triangular space left in the ashlar walls over the citadel gateway with its three great blocks of stone was filled with a limestone slab, $27^{1}/_{2}$″ thick. Its relief carving of two lions resting on the base of a central column is the first monumental relief in Greece. Such ornamentation is evidence that the cyclopean fortress walls were not only defensive, but also for show. By contrast with the Cretan palaces in their open landscape (see page 20), the mighty citadels of Greece reveal the fundamentally different mentality of their builders, and are as significant for Mycenaean culture as are the numerous weapons made for display alone (see page 35). The Homeric epics give us some idea of the life led by the native princes. Each ruled independently in his little domain, and only exceptional circumstances—such as the campaign against Troy—could bring about a temporary Panhellenic alliance.

37

Grave Circle A, Mycenae. Diameter c. 92'. Early thirteenth century B.C.

The "shaft graves" excavated by Heinrich Schliemann in 1876 were located in a circular enclosure near the Lion Gate (see page 37). Their position within the fortification walls, which deviated in order to enclose them, and their demarcation as a religious precinct justify the assumption that this "Grave Circle A" was the burial place of ancestors who were honored as heroes. The excavators found such lavish funeral offerings (see pages 34, 41, 45–48) as apparently to confirm the legend of "golden" Mycenae. Schliemann believed he had discovered the graves of famous Mycenaean heroes of Greek legend: the golden face masks that he found appeared to him to be images of Atreus or Agamemnon. A more sober present-day re-evaluation would not go quite that far; yet, on the other hand, it would not deny that these were the graves of those Greeks whose deeds prepared the ground for the flowering of Mycenaean civilization. In 1951, another burial site was found outside the fortress walls, "Grave Circle B," with similar furnishings (see page 44). This was perhaps the final resting place of a side branch of the royal house. The later form of the royal tomb was the tholos or beehive tomb (see pages 50, 51).

The fortification wall of Tiryns, which was almost twenty feet thick, was interrupted on the east by a gate and an access ramp. From here a long passageway led between the inner and outer walls to two more gateways. The ramp is so made that the unshielded side of a warrior's body would be protected by the wall. In ancient times this massive citadel was thought to be the work of the Cyclops, for it seemed impossible that the hand of man could have piled up such huge blocks of stone. The courts, halls, and reception rooms are arranged within the encircling walls in the Cretan manner.

Entrance ramp to the citadel of Tiryns. Early thirteenth century B.C.

The warrior wears a helmet of boars' tusks and carries a large shield in the shape of a figure eight. Remains of such a helmet were found in Mycenae. The image of this fully armed Mycenaean presents an aspect radically different from the Cretan ideal (see page 27). The characteristic shield, which later fell into disuse, was a popular decorative element in Mycenaean wall paintings and minor arts.

The bull's head (facing page) is of silver, the horns and the rosette on the forehead of gold. The nostrils and insides of the ears are gilded; the outside of the bronze ears and the eyes (whose pupils were once inlaid with colored material) are silvered.

Rhyton in the form of a bull's head. Silver and gold, height 12$\frac{1}{4}$" (without horns, c. 6"). Sixteenth century B.C. From shaft grave IV of Grave Circle A, Mycenae. National Museum, Athens

A very similar bull's head made of steatite was found in Knossos and fragments of another, also of steatite, were found in Mycenae. Such an impressive depiction of a bull in Mycenae is surprising, since worship of the bull was a typically Cretan phenomenon (see page 30). But since this is obviously a cult vessel, it appears that Cretan culture also influenced the religious concepts of the Greeks.

Grave stele (detail). Limestone, over-all height 52$^1/_2$″, over-all width 41$^3/_4$″. Sixteenth century B.C. Formerly over shaft grave V of Grave Circle A, Mycenae. National Museum, Athens

The spiral design of the upper field and the scene with the charioteer in the lower balance one another. Ornamentation even intrudes into the pictorial representation. Motifs of the chase and battle also decorate other grave steles from Mycenae. The nonrepresentational part of the stele may be seen as the first re-emergence of Greek ornamental design (see pages 13, 14), which here crowds out the Cretan figural art.

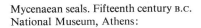

Mycenaean seals. Fifteenth century B.C.
National Museum, Athens:

"*Mistress of the Beasts.*" Impression and seal, carnelian lentoid, diameter c. ⁷/₈″. From a chamber tomb in the lower city of Mycenae

Priest and Griffin. Impression and seal, jasper lentoid, diameter c. ⁷/₈″. From the tholos tomb of Vaphio, near Sparta

Two Ducks. Impression of an onyx amygdaloid, length c. ⁵/₈″, height ³/₈″. From the tholos tomb of Vaphio, near Sparta

Cow and Calf. Impression of an onyx lentoid, diameter c. ⁷/₈″. From a chamber tomb in the lower city of Mycenae

The Cretan-Mycenaean gems, often made of striated (banded) stones, supplement what we know of this cultural epoch in almost every field. Where the subject matter fails to provide a clue, it is almost impossible to distinguish the Cretan or Mycenaean provenance of these small works of art. Itinerant craftsmen appear to have filled the surprisingly great demand for seal stones.

Funerary mask. Electrum, height $8^5/_8''$. Fifteenth century B.C. From grave Gamma of Grave Circle B, west of the Lion Gate of Mycenae. National Museum, Athens

This mask is so similar to two gold masks found in shaft grave IV of Grave Circle A (located within the fortification walls) that the hypothesis of a family relationship has been put forward. However, these masks are portraits only in a very limited sense and reproduce a given type rather than an individual. They were used as a facial covering, thus shielding the features of the deceased from the corrosive influences of time. Gold (or, in this case, electrum, a natural alloy of gold and silver) was chosen for this purpose because of its durability, and because it symbolized the passage of the dead to the status of a hero.

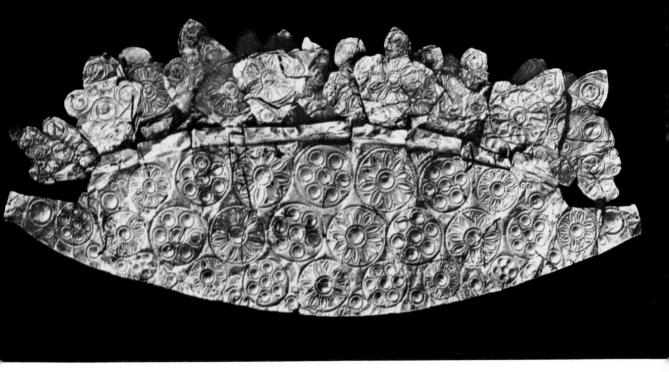

Funerary diadem. Gold foil, length 24¹/₂″. Sixteenth century B.C. From shaft grave III of Grave Circle A, Mycenae. National Museum, Athens

The pointed oval surface is stamped with an allover circular motif, while the funnel-shaped designs along the upper rim only faintly suggest their lily origin. This diadem is extremely fragile and was probably meant to be used only as an ornament for the dead. The three rows of circles (see also page 47) are so arranged on the pointed oval as to fit neatly into its form. This sense of order is a typically Greek trait.

Fighting Animals and *Spirals*. Repoussé plaques probably used as facing on a hexagonal wooden casket. Gold, length of plaques $3^5/_8''$ and $3^1/_8''$. Sixteenth century B.C. From shaft grave V of Grave Circle A, Mycenae. National Museum, Athens

The attack of a lion on a gazelle or stag seems to have dissolved into ornamental shapes and is overgrown by palmette and flower motifs. The composition of the spiral designs on the other plaque is just as important as the figural decoration (see the grave stele on page 42). Here, the conflict between Greek art and Cretan pictorial forms has reached a critical point, identifiable by this dissolution of natural forms. Late Mycenaean art transformed these into wholly abstract ornamentation (see pages 54, 56, 60).

Disks with animal and spiral ornamentation, for fastening to clothing. Gold foil, diameters c. $2-2^3/_8''$. Sixteenth century B.C. From shaft grave III of Grave Circle A, Mycenae. National Museum, Athens

The demands of symmetry have turned butterflies and octopuses into ornaments. The great decorative genius of the Greek artist expresses itself in circle, band, and spiral motifs.

Cup. Gold, height c. 5″. Sixteenth century B.C. From shaft grave V of Grave Circle A, Mycenae. National Museum, Athens

Numerous cups of precious metal have been found in the Mycenaean shaft graves. Of various shapes, some use the smooth surface of the gold to obtain their effect, others are decorated in relief or with inlays of colored metals. This simple cylindrical cup is decorated, above and below a thick dividing ring, with a double row of spiral motifs beaten in relief from the reverse side of the gold walls.

Cup with wishbone handle. Inside gold, outside silver, with bulls' heads inlaid in gold and niello, height 2¹/₄″, diameter 6¹/₈″. Early fifteenth century B.C. From a tholos tomb near Mideia (Argolis). National Museum, Athens

This cup comprised part of the funerary furnishings in the tomb of a princess, while the king was accompanied into his grave by several cups—among them one with bulls not unlike those from Vaphio (see pages 32, 33). A very similar vessel came from Enkomi on Cyprus. The form and arrangement of the bull's-head motifs here suggest that they have lost any deeper significance and serve only as ornamentation.

49

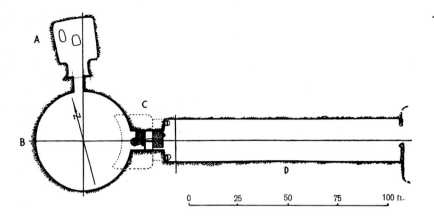

So-called Treasury of Atreus. Tholos tomb southwest of the citadel of Mycenae. Early thirteenth century B.C.

The dromos (long uncovered passageway) of the "Treasury of Atreus" is about twenty feet wide and forty yards long. Constructed of conglomerate ashlar blocks, it leads to the façade of the tomb, which was once decorated with columns and reliefs in varicolored stone. A doorway, some eighteen feet high, leads into a circular room (diameter almost forty-eight feet) covered with a corbeled, or false, dome a little more than forty-three feet high. The grave itself was located in a chamber carved out of the rock and connected to the tholos by a smaller doorway.

This tholos tomb, as well as that in Orchomenos (right), and the Lion Gate of Mycenae (see page 37) seem to be by the same architect. Prerequisite for such work was the perfection of technique such as is seen in the stonework here, for only with large and accurately cut stones could such vast areas be roofed over with corbeled vaulting. The horizontally staggered stones are laid in bands, each row projecting over the one below so as to form a dome in the shape of an old-fashioned beehive.

So-called Treasury of Minyas. Tholos tomb at Orchomenos. Width of dromos c. 20′; entrance to tholos c. 18′ high and c. 9′ wide at the base; diameter of tholos c. 46′. Early thirteenth century B.C. View from the tholos toward the dromos

Pausanias (IX, 38, 2) praised the "Treasury of Minyas" as a marvelous structure which compared favorably with any other building in Greece or elsewhere. Its similarity to the "Treasury of Atreus" is so striking that it justifies the assumption that they are by the same architect.

The almost life-sized head (facing page) is all that remains of Mycenaean large-scale sculpture in the round. Of undetermined significance, we can only say that the white skin, red lips, and the four red rosettes on forehead, chin, and cheeks seem to indicate that it is a woman. The hair lies close at the back of the head while on the forehead little curls—dark blue, like the eyes—emerge from under a broad fillet.

The form of this jug with stirrup handles and an off-center spout is typical of the Late Mycenaean period and disappeared with it. Decorative filler motifs have been inserted between the body of the highly schematized octopus and its tentacles.

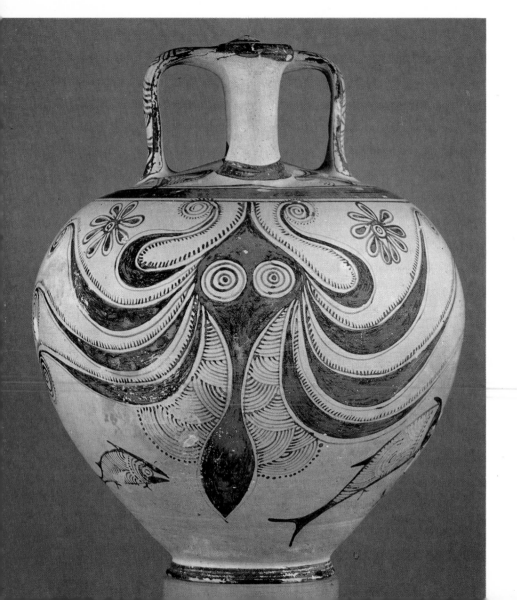

Stirrup jar. Terra cotta with glaze paint, height 8⁵/₈". Late Mycenaean, twelfth century B.C. The Metropolitan Museum of Art, New York

Head of a Woman. Painter stucco, height 6⁵/₈". Thirteenth century B.C. From Mycenae. National Museum, Athens

Pitcher. Terra cotta with glaze paint, height 7³/₄″. Late Mycenaean, thirteenth century B.C. From Ialysos (Rhodes). British Museum, London

This bulging pitcher is decorated with ten highly stylized purple-dye mollusks, recognizable as such only on the basis of numerous intermediate steps between Minoan representations and these. A corresponding development is also apparent in other motifs.

54

Grave stele. Stuccoed and painted sandstone, width of the frieze 26³/₈″. Thirteenth century B.C. From a necropolis outside Mycenae. National Museum, Athens

An incised pattern of circles lies hidden beneath the layer of stucco with its friezes of warriors and stags, indicating that the stele was used more than once. The style of painting has much in common with that of contemporary vase paintings.

Cover of an incense burner. Terra cotta with glaze paint, height 4³/₄″. Thirteenth century B.C. From Palaikastro (east coast of Crete). Archaeological Museum, Herakleion

Only the heads of the swimming ducks, whose bodies are entirely covered with ornamentation, are in any way true to life; and even they are transformed, by repetition, into a pattern. This piece of late Cretan pottery is an example of the trend toward pure ornament which occurred both here and on the Greek mainland, as well as evidence of the homogeneity of Late Mycenaean ceramic art everywhere.

The bull on this krater (mixing bowl) has retained practically nothing of the magnificent vitality of the bulls on the Vaphio cups (see pages 32, 33): here it is a mere schematized reminder, totally lacking in flesh and blood. The same figure is repeated on both sides of the vessel with only slight variations. The tendency toward an ornamental breakdown of the body is apparent in the treatment of the animal's skin.

Krater. Terra cotta with glaze paint, height 10⁵/₈″. Late Mycenaean, thirteenth century B.C. From Enkomi (Cyprus). British Museum, London

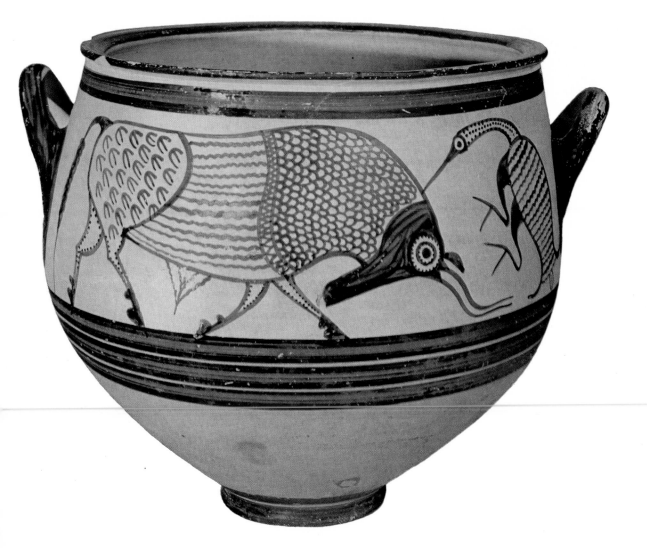

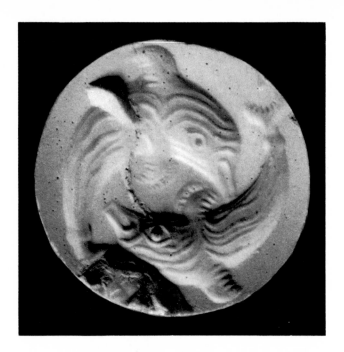

The lively, frolicking dolphins of the seal (left), which seem to chase each other in a circle and are surrounded by a play of light and water, have become a stiff and lifeless symmetrical pattern in the floor panel from Tiryns (below).

Dolphins. Jasper lentoid seal, diameter c. ³/₄″. Fifteenth century B.C. From the tholos tomb of Vaphio, near Sparta. National Museum, Athens

Dolphins. Painted floor panel of lime stucco, height of panel 23⅝″. Thirteenth century B.C. From the citadel of Tiryns (see page 39). Symmetrically arranged dolphins alternate with octopuses (similar to that shown on page 47, top right)

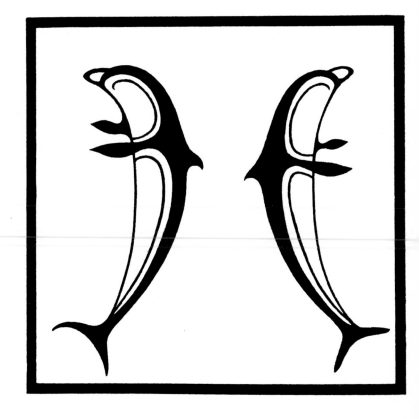

58

Female Idol. Terra cotta with glaze paint, height 4³/₄″. Thirteenth century B.C. Römisch-Germanisches Zentralmuseum, Mainz

The limited interest shown by the Mycenaean Greeks in the forms of nature is also evident in their sculpture. Representation is limited to the essential, and the lifelike statuettes of Minoan art (see page 21) are replaced by figural symbols, in some respects reminiscent of the Cycladic idols (see page 15).

A standing draped woman with her hands placed in front of her body is here depicted in the simplest possible way. Other idols of the same type have their hands uplifted, or the woman occasionally holds a child in her arms, or two women busy themselves with a child (cf. the older ivory group from Mycenae, page 36). Some of these votive offerings probably represent divinities, and some orants.

Krater. Terra cotta with glaze paint, height c. 7⁷/₈″. Late Mycenaean, twelfth century B.C. From Iria (Argolis). Archaeological Museum, Nauplia

The handle zone of this vessel is articulated in the manner of metopes or panels. Small curved lines, a no longer recognizable vestige of representational decoration, have been added to the age-old geometric motifs. This abstraction is characteristic of numerous Late Mycenaean vessels. It documents the absolute victory of Greek ornamentation over the old Minoan pictorial art—the result of a long struggle—and connects the Early and Middle Helladic with the succeeding Geometric art.

The tense forms of Geometric pottery (see page 62), its clear articulation, and the refined simplicity of the painting testify to the delight of the potter in the technical inventions of the potter's wheel and glaze paint, which had been in use from Mycenaean times. The close relationship between the form of the vessel and its decoration, which was to remain characteristic throughout the Geometric period, reveals the strict discipline of the Greek artist.

GEOMETRIC ART (1100–700 B.C.)

The "Doric migrations" signified the end of the Mycenaean world. Palaces and citadels fell before the flood tide of the Greek tribes penetrating from the North. The second wave of Greek immigration brought with it a new social order which narrowed the gulf between the princes of the Mycenaean citadels and their peasant subjects. Patriarchal customs based on peasant tradition now prevailed, leaving the nobility only a slight edge of superiority. Some of the Mycenaean Achaians probably emigrated; in some regions of Greece they found ways of coexistence with their new masters. Tradition recounts that Athens was spared from these upheavals, and here Geometric art attained an early and individual flowering. It is thus clear that Geometric art was not brought in by the immigrants as a finished product but that the new life infused by the newcomers into Greek art as the Mycenaean culture came to an end provided the necessary impetus for the full develop-

ment and diffusion of Greek ornamental art. Finds from the Dipylon cemetery (whence the name "Dipylon vases") display the continuing traditions of the Athenian potters at the time of the Doric migrations. The transition from Late Mycenaean to Geometric pottery took place gradually, without the intervening crises that political revolution must inevitably bring.

Amphora. Terra cotta with glaze paint, height 15³/₄″. Protogeometric, tenth century B.C. From the cemetery south of the Eridanos, Athens. Kerameikos Museum, Athens

◀ Amphora. Terra cotta with glaze paint, height 27³/₈″. Protogeometric, first half of ninth century B.C. From the Dipylon cemetery, Athens. Kerameikos Museum, Athens

A symmetry, enlivened by small variations, reigns in the "metope" frieze of the handle area. The decoration articulates the vessel into dark and light zones, which accentuate the egg shape of the body of the vase as well as the sweep of the high neck.

Amphora (detail). Terra cotta with glaze paint, height 61″. Geometric, c. 770 B.C. From the Dipylon cemetery. National Museum, Athens

The detail shows a mourning scene with the corpse on its bier in the center; only the two figures at the far left are identified as men by their weapons. On the reverse of the vessel another small panel with more mourning figures is reserved in the bands of geometric ornament which encircle the entire vessel. On the neck are two narrow friezes of deer among the bands of ornamental motifs.

This first appearance of human and animal figures was preceded by a long period of pure Geometric art (see pages 61, 62). Yet by their very shapes, even these figural elements have become ornaments.

Krater. Terra cotta with glaze paint, height 48³/₈″. Geometric, mid-eighth century B.C. National Museum, Athens

The two wide figural friezes with their representations of a magnificent funeral cortege and of a long row of warriors in their chariots have, to a large extent, replaced the pure ornament. The band of two-horse chariots seems to indicate races held in honor of the deceased.

Krater (detail). Terra cotta with glaze paint, height of the frieze 3⁷/₈″. Geometric, eighth century B.C. The Metropolitan Museum of Art, New York

Geometric pictorial art, as it were in competition with the narrative epic poetry, developed in a wealth of figural representations whose heroes have mostly remained nameless. Above is a naval battle, while below two lions are seen devouring a man; to the left of them is a battle scene and, to the right, are a lyre player and women carrying jugs on their heads.

Kantharos (detail). Terra cotta with glaze paint, height of the frieze 1⁵/₈″. Late Geometric, late eighth century B.C. From the Dipylon cemetery, Athens. National Museum, Copenhagen

Two Warriors Fighting for a Tripod. Fragment of the foot of a tripod. Bronze, height 18$^1/_2$″, width 3$^3/_4$″. Eighth century B.C. From Olympia. Archaeological Museum, Olympia

Proof that Geometric art was not only a potter's art is provided by incised patterns on utensils of various kinds, engravings on the catchplates of fibulae (see page 72), and embossed and cast reliefs on bronze implements. The flat supporting legs of tripods are usually decorated only with ornamental motifs, and figural representations such as that on the left are rare exceptions. Although both men wear helmets and are undifferentiated, the event shown is undoubtedly the struggle between Herakles and Apollo. In the lower panel two rampant lions face each other. The vertical ridges found on other tripod legs have here been modified on account of the intervening figural panels.

Nude Goddess. Ivory statuette, height 9¹/₂". 750–725 B.C. From a Geometric vessel found in the Dipylon cemetery, which also contained four other ivory figurines of nude goddesses. National Museum, Athens

Both the general sculptural form and the material of which it is made would indicate an Eastern origin for the little figurine on the right. However, the rationally understood construction of the human figure suffices to reveal the artist as Greek; while additional proof is provided by the Greek meander on the polos (divine crown). The statuette would thus seem to be a precursor of the sculptural creations of the Archaic period (see pages 77, 91).

Bird. Terra cotta with glaze paint, length 6¹/₄". c. 750 B.C. From the cemetery south of the Eridanos, Athens. Kerameikos Museum, Athens

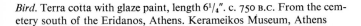

Hero and Centaur. Bronze, height 4³/₈″. Eighth century B.C. Purportedly from Olympia. The Metropolitan Museum of Art, New York

The mother suckling its young is a favorite motif of Geometric small-scale sculpture. The bird sitting on the rump of the animal—which is female, despite the large antlers—emphasizes the idyllic aspect of this scene taken from nature. A relief meander on the underside of the base indicates that the object was not fixed, but was meant to be held in the hand and looked at from every angle.

◄ The hero, wearing a helmet like the centaur, stands on an extension of the openwork base of the latter. Their interlocked arms are probably intended to indicate fighting rather than friendly greeting. The battle with the centaur—a hybrid creature of horse and man—in which the extremes of beastly nature and human culture are reflected, is a favorite theme in Greek art and appears in vase paintings (see pages 73, 93, 134), temple metopes (see page 152), pediments (see page 134), and in large-scale painting. The centaur legend is connected with Herakles (who killed Nessos) and Achilles (who was taught by the wise Chiron). The most famous centauromachy resulted from the brutish behavior of the centaurs at Peirithoös' wedding (see page 134).

Horse. Bronze, height c. 4³/₄". Eighth century B.C. National Museum, Athens

Geometric animal figurines are preponderantly in the form of horses, although bulls and birds also exist. Evidently they are votive offerings which were deposited in sanctuaries. Some were apparently suspended so that the undersides—frequently decorated—could be seen. There was a tendency toward an exaggeration of the slenderness of the extremities and trunk in the horse figurines: the powerful parts of the animal are depicted as massive shapes, while the thinness of the connecting parts and joints is stressed. Despite their apparent lack of realism, these rather manneristic forms succeed in putting across a very vivid picture of the nature of the horse.

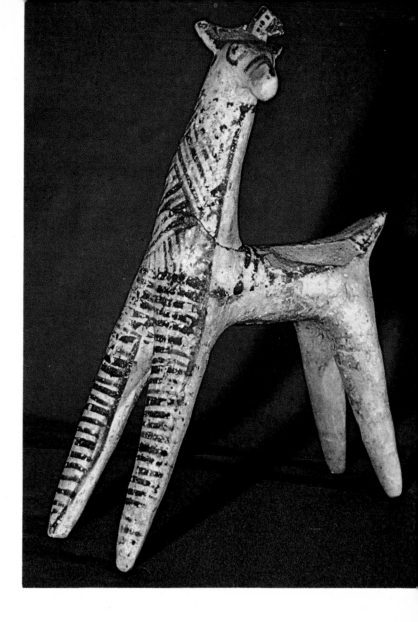

Horse. Painted terra cotta, height 7½″. Late eighth century B.C. Antikensammlung, Munich

Countless terra-cotta horses such as this, unpretentious in comparison with the bronze statuettes, were used as votive offerings or as funeral gifts to be laid in the tomb. Their style, like the material, is simple, but they are enriched with ornamental painting. Surprising here in this otherwise rather stiff little horse is the momentary turn of the head.

These Geometric animal figurines are the first in a long series of Greek representations of animals. While many examples from the Archaic age have survived (see pages 80, 81), little is known of the famous animal sculptures of the classical age.

Four fibulae. Gold, heights $2^3/_8$″ and $1^7/_8$″. c. 700 B.C. British Museum, London

The two larger pins have a swastika on one side of the catchplate and a deer on the other; the smaller ones are decorated with animal pictures and a ship. More often the fibulae are of bronze and are sometimes very large. The scenes engraved on the catchplates frequently represent mythological events.

THE SEVENTH CENTURY B.C.

The horizon of the Greeks expanded as colonies were established on almost all the coasts of the Mediterranean during the second half of the eighth and the seventh centuries B.C. Greek Geometric art seemed stiff and backward compared with the art of the East, and some aspects of the latter were accepted as worthy of imitation. The crisis which Greek art faced can be surmised from the great endeavors made in the new fields of monumental sculpture and painting. The cornerstone for subsequent Greek art was laid in this time of unrest.

In the principal scene on this amphora Herakles, preparing to punish the centaur Nessos, dismounts from a chariot in which Deianeira is seated. On the neck of the jar a lion attacks a deer, and in the shoulder zone two grazing horses are depicted. The figural decoration is confined to the front of the vase, which is clearly differentiated from the back. The pliability of the figures and the flexibility of the ornamentation contrast sharply with the rigid Geometric style. In this same period pots painted in the old tradition were still being produced alongside those which had decisively broken with Geometric traditions.

Amphora. Terra cotta with glaze paint, height 36⁵/₈″. Proto-Attic, early seventh century B.C. The Metropolitan Museum of Art, New York

The Trojan Horse, detail of a relief amphora. Terra cotta, over-all height 49$^{1}/_{4}$″, height of the scene shown c. 12$^{1}/_{2}$″. Cycladic, seventh century B.C. From Mykonos. Museum, Mykonos

The scene on the neck of this amphora is the largest of a series of twenty pictures narrating the story of the fall of Troy. The other scenes are arranged in three tiers on the body of the vessel (on the front side only). This detail shows the Greek heroes looking out of the hatches in the wooden horse and handing out weapons and armor to their comrades who have already dismounted. The jar belongs to a class of monumental relief amphorae which were produced only in the seventh century B.C. They show the trend toward large size prevalent even in the pottery of this period. The center of production was in the Cyclades.

Krater. Terra cotta with glaze paint and red color, height 37³/₈″. Cycladic, c. 660 B.C. From Melos. National Museum, Athens

A duel witnessed by women is painted on the front of the neck of this krater. The principal scene is of Apollo in his four-horse chariot; standing in the chariot behind him are two women (Muses?); and Artemis comes to meet him. Two horses stand in the center of the reverse side, while the remaining surface is covered with ornamental motifs. The foot shows a woman's head in each of the metope-like panels. Like the relief vessels (see page 74), these painted Cycladic vases are also characterized by a monumental tendency which clearly differentiates them from the preference for small scale evident in the Corinthian paintings (see pages 83, 84).

This example of early Attic painting supplements the information supplied by painted vases (see page 93). In both cases a largeness and simplicity of line quite equal to that of Cycladic painting (see pages 74, 75) is evident. In its broad handling the Attic picture is evidence of the fact that painting has outgrown the limits set by the ceramic technique, and that monumental painting is on its way to becoming an independent art form (see page 135). The bearded god on the left appears to be receiving the lyre held by a figure on the right. The latter is almost entirely missing and is of uncertain identification—perhaps Leto. Originally the picture must have measured about twenty by twenty-four inches and may have been an independent painting or a temple metope.

Goddesses (Leto and Artemis?). Hammered bronze, height 15³/₄″ and 17³/₄″. Cretan, mid-seventh century B.C. From Dreros (Crete). Archaeological Museum, Herakleion

These female statuettes, found with that of a god (31¹/₂″ high) in the temple of Dreros, probably represent Leto and Artemis. (Apollo was apparently worshiped here together with his mother and sister.) The figures are made by the *sphyrelaton* technique, that is, they are assembled of hammered sheets of bronze nailed over a wooden core. This method permitted the creation of bronze statues of considerable size at a time when hollow bronze casting was still unknown. The figures give the impression of having been carved out of tree trunks and clearly show their affinity to the wood sculpture that was so important in earlier times, although they are also reminiscent of the Geometric ivory figure (see page 67).

Two lions lie side by side on a rectangular slab, their heads protruding over the corners. Between them stands a goddess holding the ends of leashes which pass around the necks of the lions. On the hindquarters of each lion stands a somewhat smaller female figure holding the other end of the leash and the animal's tail. Similar supports made of the same Lakonian marble were found in Olympia, Rhodes, and Corinth. They may have

Caldron stand. Blue-gray marble with red paint, height 20¹/₂″. First half of seventh century B.C. From the Heraion of Samos. State Museums, Berlin

come from a Spartan workshop. The self-contained form of the female figures relates them to the bronze goddesses of Dreros (see page 77) and characterized the "Daidalic" style, which was named after the legendary sculptor Daidalos. It originated in the seventh century B.C. and spread throughout Greece.

Head of a Goddess, detail of the vertical handle of a hydria. Bronze, height of handle 6⁷/₈", height of head 2³/₈". Spartan, early sixth century B.C. From Livadia (Boeotia). Archäologisches Institut der Universität, Mainz

The inscription TELESSTAS scratched into the rim of the mouth of this hydria makes it appear likely that it was made by the Spartan sculptor whose statue of Zeus at Olympia is mentioned by Pausanias (V, 23, 7). The style of this little head also suggests Sparta, where—contrary to popular belief—numerous works of art were created. The practicing artists were, however, not members of that ruling warrior caste upon which our notion of ancient Sparta is based. For a brief span of time the craftsmen who created the Spartan vases might have been Mothakes (children of Spartan fathers and Helot mothers) or Helots (slaves of the state), assuming that they even belonged to the Spartan Confederation as less privileged members. For larger artistic undertakings foreign artists were called in.

Lion. Naxian marble, height 58¹/₄″. Late seventh century B.C. Delos, processional way to the sacred lake

From Late Geometric times on, the king of beasts was frequently represented as a terrifying, murderous creature (see pages 65, 66). The lion was not indigenous to Greece and was therefore treated like legendary creatures such as the griffin and the sphinx, which appeared alongside other animals on vases. The crouching lion of Corfu (facing page) is probably a funerary monument, since it was found in a necropolis. The concept of a lion as a tomb guardian is widespread and is supported by an epigram: "I am the strongest of wild beasts. I have mounted this stone burial place of the dead, over whom I keep watch."

In Delos, nine seated lions flank the Sacred Way. The idea of such "avenues" may stem from the Orient, especially from Egypt, while their construction shows the independence of the artists and their striving for monumentality with its inherent danger of extravagance. Of the gigantic statues hewn out of the famous marble of the Cycladic islands some remained unfinished in the quarries, their dimensions having exceeded the limits of the possible. One such colossus would have been thirty-six feet high.

◀ *Lion*. Grayish-yellow limestone, over-all length of base 48″. Late seventh century B.C. From Corfu, near the tomb of Menekrates. Museum, Corfu

Drinking cup (skyphos). Terra cotta with glaze paint and white and red color, height 7½″. Proto-Corinthian, early seventh century B.C. From Kameiros (Rhodes). British Museum, London

The figure of a running dog decorates the front and reverse of this skyphos; under the handles are a goose and a palmette bow. While Proto-Corinthian vase painting generally tended toward miniature work, here it shows a surprising largeness of form despite the small size of the vessel. The products of Corinthian potters were greatly in demand and were distributed by tradesmen to the far corners of the Greek world.

This little masterpiece of the early Corinthian potter's art shows, arranged in three tiers, a colorful battle scene, a horse race, and a hare hunt. The mouth of the vessel is in the form of a lion's head. Except for its wider neck, the jar has the shape of an early type of lekythos and was used as a perfume container. Such recipients for aromatic oils are often entirely or partly in the shape of a human figure or an animal (see pages 100, 105).

Perfume flask (aryballos). Terra cotta with glaze paint and white and red color, height 2⁵/₈″. Proto-Corinthian, mid-seventh century B.C. From Thebes. British Museum, London

This jug is the most important extant example of early Corinthian painting. Shown in three friezes are: the approach of two armies preparing for battle; a procession of horsemen, chariots, a lion hunt, and the Judgment of Paris; and in the bottom frieze, a hare hunt. A lotus design has been painted with opaque color on top of the glaze paint around the mouth of the jug, and a row of running animals has been similarly painted on the band of glaze paint beneath the first frieze. The pictures do not seem to be related to each other in subject matter. Only in the scene of the Judgment of Paris have the names of the figures been inscribed. The artist exhibits his talent in the delicacy of his figures, in their colorful nature, in their lifelike portrayal, and in their grouping, while their true meaning seems to be of secondary importance.

Jug (olpe), the so-called *Chigi Vase*. Terra cotta with dark and light glaze paint and red and white color, height 10¹/₄". Proto-Corinthian, c. 640 B.C. From Formello, near Veii (Italy). Villa Giulia, Rome

Kneeling Youth. Ivory with amber inlay, height 5³/₄". c. 630 B.C. From the Heraion of Samos. Museum, Samos

Together with a companion piece, this nude kneeling youth supported the arms of a lyre that belonged to the temple treasure of Hera. The figure is frontally oriented, although it would primarily have been seen from the side; the head has a slight twist to the left, probably because it was attached to the right side of the lyre. The complete nudity of the figure and the broad, tightly drawn metal belt mark the work as Greek. The inlay technique suggests, however, that the Greek artist had learned ivory carving from an Eastern master. The eyes, eyebrows, and pubic hair were inlaid with different colored material, and remains of amber have been preserved in the locks of hair on the brow. It is also possible that a Near Eastern ivory worker may have adapted himself to the Greek way of life and have executed this costly musical instrument in Greek style. Such adaptation must frequently have taken place as a result of the wandering mode of life which the ivory carvers are known to have led. Furthermore, the idea of decorating a musical instrument with sculptural figures also seems to be of Oriental origin.

Duel over a Corpse. Terra-cotta plate with glaze paint and white and purple colors over a cream slip, diameter 15″. Rhodian, late seventh century B.C. From Kameiros (Rhodes). British Museum, London

Like Corinth, Melos (see page 75), and Athens, Rhodes also had its own pottery workshops. Its highly decorative products are usually ornamented with several rows of animals: mythological scenes are rarer. On this plate, the inscriptions indicate that Menelaos and Hektor are fighting over the corpse of Euphorbos. Rich ornamental motifs encroach upon the picture, which fills the bowl of the plate but for a small lower segment.

The eyes painted on either side of the pendant volute pattern lend an air of fantasy to the scene. In the *Iliad* (XVII) Homer describes how Menelaos defeated Euphorbos and robbed him of his armor and weapons. The shield of Euphorbos was later exhibited in the Heraion of Argos as a sacrificial offering of Menelaos (Pausanias, II, 17, 3). There is no evidence that Hektor took part in this battle.

"Mantiklos dedicated me as his tithe to the far-striking god with the silver bow. Do thou, O Phoebus, grant him his desired reward." So reads the inscription on this little bronze figure of Apollo. Any attempt to identify this Mantiklos with the hero of the second Mycenaean War is thwarted by the Boeotian character of the inscription. Were it only a matter of dating, an identification would be quite possible. In its articulated structure this figure, nude but for a tight bronze belt, heralds the imminent approach of the kouros figure in large-scale sculpture. The frontally oriented, inflexible posture is that of a monumental statue, and this statuette may be a copy of a large cult image.

The nude male figure dominates Archaic sculpture and, generally speaking, this was to remain so in later Greek art. However, it would be erroneous to conclude that the nudity of these figures simply represents a custom of the early Greeks carried over into art. To be sure, a freer attitude toward nudity was common in Greece, but in daily life the wearing of clothes was taken for granted. The fact that, in the gymnasiums and in the great Olympic contests, athletes competed in the nude, as also the care applied to the development of the body, shows that the beauty of the human figure was revealed to the Greeks in its nudity. Only undraped does the human body reveal its logical structure—the functioning of its individual parts as well as the co-ordination of its appendages. These were the characteristics that mattered more to the sculptor than mere outer appearance.

Apollo. Statuette dedicated to the god by Mantiklos. Bronze, height 8″. Boeotian, early seventh century B.C. From Thebes. Museum of Fine Arts, Boston

In small-scale sculpture the human figure, ever since the Geometric period, showed an astonishing propensity for movement—albeit of a puppetlike kind. Large-scale sculpture, however, followed quite different paths (see pages 89 ff.).

Warrior. Bronze statuette, height 8″. Early seventh century B.C. From the Acropolis, Athens. National Museum, Athens

Warrior. Bronze statuette, height 6⁷/₈″. Late seventh century B.C. From Olympia. Museum, Olympia

This youth stands erect and in a frontal pose, his left foot advanced and his fists pressed to his thighs. While the complete nudity of the statue and the absence of any support differentiate it from Egyptian antecedents, the basic idea of large-scale sculpture, as well as other elements, are of Egyptian derivation. There was no direct development from the older bronze statuettes (facing page) to the often over life-size kouroi. The kouros figure was a distinct basic type which prevailed until about 500 B.C. and which was constructed according to specific rules, which nonetheless permitted infinite variations according to period, location, and artist. Simultaneously there was a trend toward an ever better grasp of anatomic details. The kouros in New York, which probably stood on the grave of a young Attic aristocrat, seems particularly slender and noble in contrast with the contemporary statues of Kleobis and Biton (see page 90). It embodies the current Athenian ideal of beauty.

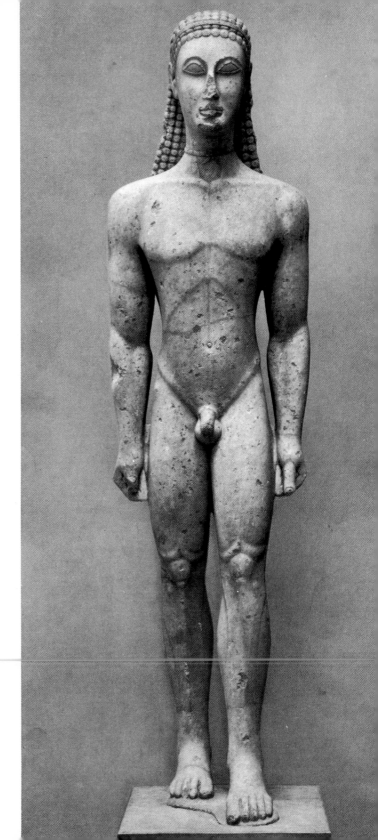

Kouros. Marble, height 6′ 4″. Late seventh century B.C. From Attica. The Metropolitan Museum of Art, New York

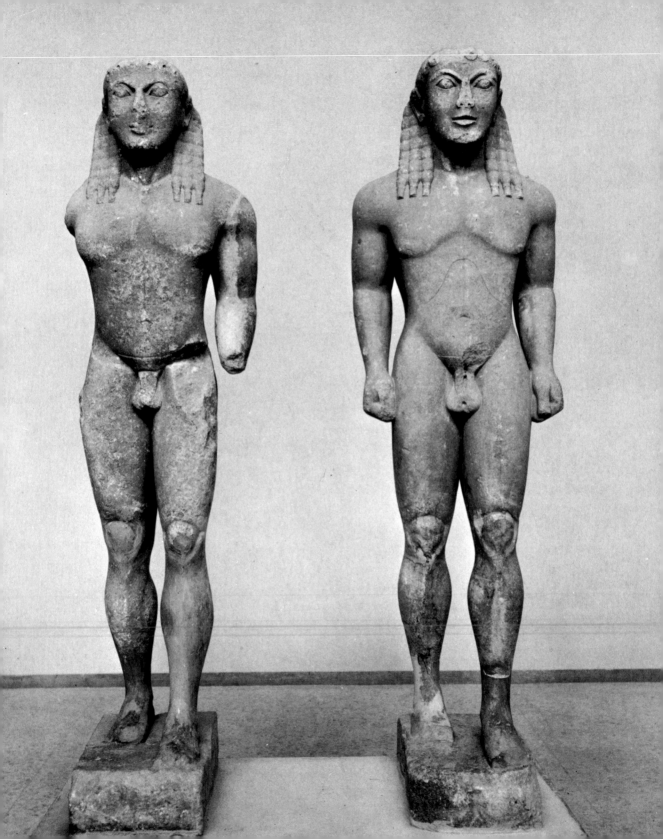

Kleobis and Biton, by Polymedes of Argos. Marble, height 86″ and 85″. Late seventh century B.C. From Delphi. Museum, Delphi

The inscription on the upper side of the plinths, in which the artist also identifies himself, states that the two statues represent Kleobis and Biton, heroes whose feats are recounted by Herodotos (I, 31) and others. When the oxen which were to pull the chariot of their mother, the priestess Kydippe, to the Heraion of Argos failed to arrive, her sons took the shafts themselves. They were rewarded by being granted a peaceful and early death in sleep. Herodotus also mentions these statues, which he himself probably saw. The concentrated vigor of the figures, so clearly different from the Attic elegance of the New York kouros (see page 89), apparently corresponds to the Doric ideal, but is also motivated here by the young men's heroic deed.

The pomegranate which she holds in her right hand does not suffice to identify the "*Standing Goddess of Berlin*" (right). She could be Persephone or Aphrodite. However, the polos on her head (see pages 67, 77) definitely shows her to be a goddess. She seems the female counterpart of the New York kouros (see page 89); but while the kouros type had already reached its definitive form, the kore (maiden) statue so characteristic of Archaic times did not develop until later (see pages 109, 114 ff.). In earlier times, body and garments formed a single columnar or slab-shaped unit (see pages 77, 78).

Goddess. Marble with bluish-gray veins, abundant traces of original painting, height 77″. Attic, early sixth century B.C. From Keratea (Attica). State Museums, Berlin

Kouros. Marble, height c. 10′. c. 600 B.C. From Sounion (Attica). National Museum, Athens

Because of its monumental size, this statue, which was found in the vicinity of the temple in the foothills of Sounion together with other fragments, seems more self-contained than the smaller, possibly contemporary, kouros of New York (see page 89). These colossi stood in an enclosure consecrated to Poseidon and were visible from afar to seafarers. Here the god had only an altar, and as yet no temple.

Amphora showing Herakles and Nessos. Terra cotta with glaze paint and (originally) red and white color, height 48″. Late seventh century B.C. From the Dipylon cemetery, Athens. National Museum, Athens

This monumental amphora is painted only on the front side. The battle with the centaur on the neck includes the inscription of the names "Herakles" and "Netos" (Nessos). On the body of the vessel the decapitated Medusa is depicted with her sisters, who are pursuing Perseus, although the figure of the hero is not shown. The picture on the neck has the same largeness of drawing as the Attic panel painting (see page 76). The uncertainty, hesitancy, and experimentation of older Attic vase paintings (see page 73) have yielded to a confident self-awareness that enabled Attic pottery to overshadow the Corinthian. The latter now lost its market and rapidly declined.

Enthroned Goddesses. Terra cotta with cream-colored ground and ceramic colors, formerly c. $31^{1}/_{2} \times 31^{1}/_{2}''$. Corinthian, late seventh century B.C. Metope from a temple in Thermon (Aetolia). National Museum, Athens

The painted metope above, framed on either side by a frieze of rosettes, shows three enthroned goddesses, perhaps the Charites (Graces). The rich ornamentation of the throne and robes indicates that the metope was restored at a later date (probably in the third century B.C.). Other surviving metopes of this temple depict scenes of Greek legend. Since these "panel paintings" are our only evidence, apart from vase paintings, for the Corinthian art of this period, they are particularly significant. Greek tradition allots an important place in the history of Greek painting to Corinth.

THE SIXTH CENTURY B.C.

In its encounter with that of the Orient, the art of Greece preserved its independence and Archaic art now took on its characteristic form. Art quietly set itself specific goals and strove for greater naturalism and increased subtlety of individual details within these given limits. The relative straightforwardness of Archaic art was also reflected in contemporary life. The rule of the tyrants was established as the prevailing form of government and the splendid court life maintained by the rulers led to the formulation of universal modes of living. Philosophy sought out the laws of nature; morality was determined by the rules of life of the sages.

Pitcher (oinochoe). Terra cotta with glaze paint and white and red color, height 9⁷/₈″. Attic, early sixth century B.C. From the Athenian Agora. Agora Museum, Athens

The picture of a swan beating its wings sweeps across the panel reserved in the light color of the clay on the right side of this pitcher. In Attic vase painting, the combination of Cycladic monumentality (see page 75) with Corinthian delicacy (see pages 83, 84) results in a restrained largeness which infuses a living tension into every image.

Temple of Apollo, Corinth. Limestone. Mid-sixth century B.C. The seven surviving columns of the northwest corner

This Doric temple was provided on the west and east with porches, had two cellae (indicating that in addition to Apollo, a second divinity—Artemis?—was honored), and was surrounded by a colonnade six columns wide at the front and fifteen at the sides. The shafts of the columns (almost twenty feet high) are monolithic. The stylobate, the platform on which the columns rest (70′ 6″ × 176′ 6″), was given a convex curve three-quarters of an inch high in the center in order to relieve the otherwise dead straight line. The Greek temple—the house of the god rather than a gathering place for believers—originated in its classic form in the early Archaic period, maintaining its characteristics almost unchanged through the centuries. The Doric order is the oldest, the Ionic (see pages 166, 170) soon followed, and the Corinthian made its appearance about 400 B.C. The period in which a temple was built is revealed primarily by the proportions of its columns (which become increasingly slender, see pages 117, 120, 150, 156, 157), as well as in the individual details of the ground plan and by the style of the sculptural decoration. The Greek temple sets the place for the image of the god apart from the rest of the world, yet links it once more with the environment by its columns. The sanctuary may be said to stand within the sacred enclosure like a Greek statue.

Kouros (so-called *Apollo of Tenea*). Marble, height 5'. Corinthian, mid-sixth century B.C. From Tenea, near Corinth. Glyptothek, Munich

This barely life-sized statue of a youth (see page 89) stood over a grave as a representation of a man who died in early age. The elegance of the figure seems to agree with the fineness of form in Corinthian vase paintings. The statue reached Munich in 1853, and through it both Archaic art and the kouros type (then identified as "Apollo") came to be widely known. The "Archaic smile" was at the time taken as an indication of the lack of skill of the ancient sculptor. However, the cheerful expression of the face, which is a characteristic of almost all later Archaic works, is today interpreted as a sign of the intellect which distinguished the free man, and of an openness which is entirely Greek and which it would be futile to seek in Oriental works.

The Calf Bearer. Marble, limestone base, height 65". Attic, c. 570 B.C. From the Acropolis, Athens. Acropolis Museum, Athens

According to the dedicatory inscription, the statue represents a certain [?Rh]ombos who, despite his fine clothing, is shown as a kindly herdsman. He may have been a wealthy stockbreeder who rendered thanks to the goddess Athena with his statue. The bull calf is astonishing for its lifelike expression, the statue as a whole for the harmony of man and animal. It should be noted that this older man is shown clothed (see pages 87 ff.): as the likeness of a living person he is depicted in everyday dress.

This enthroned couple, behind whom a ▶ snake is coiled, probably represents heroized dead, at whose feet small figures of worshipers bear votive offerings. The relief originally decorated a grave. Both the irregular shape of the stele and the angularity of the figures are surprising. These facts may be interpreted as a sign of provincialism, for in the course of the sixth century B.C. the once impressive artistic production of Sparta (see page 79) declined rapidly.

Heroized Dead. Relief in grayish-blue marble, ▶ height 34 1/4". Spartan, mid-sixth century B.C. From Chrysapha, near Sparta. State Museums, Berlin

Plastic vase in the form of the bust of a young woman. Terra cotta with glaze paint and white and red color, height 4³/₄″. Rhodian, mid-sixth century B.C. From Vulci (Etruria). British Museum, London

Krater. Terra cotta with glaze paint and white and red color, height 15″ (with lid, 18⁵/₈″). Chalkidian, c. 540 B.C. From Vulci (Etruria). University Museum, Würzburg

This vessel, which once contained scented oil, is in the form of a female bust of the kore type (see page 114). The chiton has been reserved in the color of the clay ground; the slanting mantle is black. On the necklace hangs a pendant in the shape of a bull's head. Figural vessels were particularly popular in Corinth (see page 83) and in the Greek East, as well as in Athens (see page 105). In them potters and sculptors could give their imagination free reign.

The scene on the front of this krater shows Hektor and Paris taking leave of Andromache and Helen. The groom Kebriones is also identified by an inscription. On the reverse are shown two horsemen, and under the handles are men running. An animal frieze ornaments the lid. Chalkidian vases are distinguished by their excellent technique, good spatial division, and balanced ornamental effect. Pottery from Chalkis (Euboea), which prospered for a short period after the middle of the sixth century, was particularly popular in Etruria, along with Corinthian and Attic products. The form of the letters in the inscriptions identifies the vase as Chalkidian.

Amphora in Fikellura style. Terra cotta with glaze paint and white color, height $13^1/_8$". Rhodian, c. 540 B.C. From Kameiros (Rhodes). British Museum, London

On the front, the large empty space is filled by the figure of a running man and, on the back, by a running hare. The guilloche pattern around the front of the neck has a corresponding meander band on the reverse. This group of vases, which takes its name from the type site on Rhodes, differs technically from other Greek black-figure vases in that the internal details of the figures are not incised with a needle but have been reserved in the ground.

Dionysos in a Ship. Cup (kylix) by Exekias. Terra cotta with glaze paint on a coral-red glaze ground and white and purple color, diameter 11³/₄". Attic, c. 540 B.C. From Vulci (Etruria). Antikensammlung, Munich

Dionysos' ship, decorated at the bow with the head of a wild boar and with the head of a swan at the stern, races full sail over a sea filled with playing dolphins. A vine twines around the mast and fills the upper part of the picture area with thick clusters of grapes. Dionysos lies alone in his ship, holding a large drinking horn. The signature of Exekias runs along the rim of the foot. Exekias, who was one of the outstanding Athenian potters and painters, was the first to present rich figural scenes from legend in a unified pictorial form; and in this sense his "compositions" have rightly been considered the starting point of Western painting.

Nike. Marble, height 35³/₈". Cycladic, c. 540 B.C. From Delos. National Museum, Athens

Curiously flattened, the goddess of victory turns her head toward the observer as she floats past. (Only the attachments of the large sickle-shaped wings remain.) The sculptor Archermos of Chios is said to have been the first to represent the victory goddess winged; and since an inscription bearing this signature was found nearby, this running-flying Nike may be presumed to be the work of Archermos, one of the outstanding sculptors of his time. The fact that he signed his work would testify to his pride in it.

Perfume flask in the form of a kneeling youth. Terra cotta with glaze paint and red color, height 10″. Attic, c. 540 B.C. From the Athenian Agora. Agora Museum, Athens

This kneeling boy, on whose head is the mouth of the flask, must have once held the ends of a ribbon threaded through the small holes in his hands (as in the photograph), thus permitting the owner of the jar to carry it around his wrist. Of its kind (see pages 83, 100), this vase is of a particularly high sculptural quality. It is therefore almost easier to evaluate it as a piece of sculpture, since we have lost the naïveté necessary for an appreciation of the object as a vessel.

Funeral Lamentation. Fragment of panels lining a tomb (?). Clay with glaze paint and red color, height 14″. Attic, c. 530 B.C. From Spata (Attica). Vlastos Collection, Athens

The style of these "panel paintings" identifies them as the work of the vase painter Lydos. He was a contemporary of Exekias (see page 103) and probably came from Asia Minor. In the potters' quarter of Athens he was known as "the Lydian," and it was thus that he signed his works, countless examples of which have survived. The activity of foreign artists in Athens and their complete identification with the art of the city testify to the irresistible pull of this cultural center.

Mother and Child. Fragment of a grave relief (detail).
Marble, height 15¹/₄". From Anavyssos (Attica). National
Museum, Athens

Only the profile of the mother and her hand lovingly cradling the head of the child have remained of this
image of a mother and child. The theme makes its first appearance here and was not to reappear until much
later. After the older form of a pillar topped by a sphinx had gone out of fashion, Attic grave steles generally
showed the image of the deceased in profile, either painted or in relief.

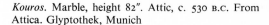

Kouros. Marble, height 82″. Attic, c. 530 B.C. From Attica. Glyptothek, Munich

With great skill the sculptor has succeeded in so balancing the tremendous weight of the statue that the slender lower legs alone were able to support the figure without any additional struts. This Attic kouros (see page 89) embodies a specific athletic ideal and the way the muscles are reproduced, the rounder modeling in comparison to older kouroi, and the substitution of the long hair with a style better adapted to sports activities, identify it as a relatively late work.

Kore. Marble with red, green, and black painting, height 46¹/₂″. Attic, c. 530 B.C. From the Athenian Acropolis. Acropolis Museum, Athens

This statue of a girl dressed in chiton and peplos comes from the "Persian fill" (see pages 127, 128) of the Acropolis. The preservation of the paint is a result of its premature destruction and early burial. The metal decoration (earrings, wreath, fibula) has been lost. Within the series of korai (maidens), this *Peplos Kore* in her modesty seems a forerunner of the later peplos figures of the fifth century, yet the contained columnar shape of the lower part of her body still relates her to the older female statues (see pages 77, 78, 91).

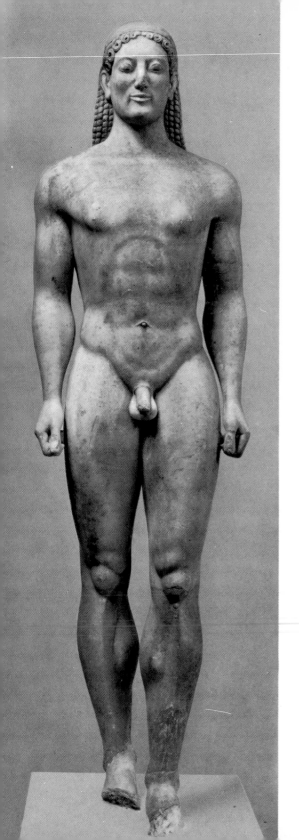

Kroisos. Marble with traces of red paint, height 76³/₈". Attic, c. 520 B.C. From Anavyssos (Attica). National Museum, Athens

An inscription on the three-stepped base addresses the beholder: "Stand and mourn by the grave of dead Kroisos, whom violent Ares snatched up from among the warriors in the front line."

The fact that an Attic youth bears the name of the Lydian king is an indication of the close ties which the Peisistratid tyranny maintained with the Oriental ruling houses.

The inscription is also significant in that it reveals that the statue stood on the grave of a young man (see page 97). Death in combat, an unusual fate, is the reason for setting up an image of eternal youth as compensation for a life cut short.

The vase on the facing page is signed both front and back by Taleides. On one side it shows the battle of Theseus with the Minotaur in the presence of the Attic youths and maidens whom he is rescuing from the Labyrinth; and on the other, a scene in which three men are occupied with a large pair of scales. This has the character of an event from daily life. Interest in such genre scenes was only beginning and the painter predominantly turned to stories from Greek mythology. Even the land and sea battles depicted on Geometric pottery are probably stories of old (see page 65). Attic black-figure vase painting was primarily concerned with the legendary deeds and heroes of which the poets sang, and these were set down with the utmost clarity which, in turn, was accentuated by the inclusion of inscriptions.

Amphora signed by Taleides. Terra cotta with glaze paint and white and red color, height 11³/₄". Attic, c. 530 B.C. From Agrigento, Sicily. The Metropolitan Museum of Art, New York

Phineus Cup. Terra cotta with glaze paint and white and red color, height 16″, diameter c. 15″. The surface is partly corroded. Chalkidian, c. 520 B.C. From Vulci (Etruria). University Museum, Würzburg

This cup, already repaired in Antiquity, has a Silenus mask in the center and, on the outside, two pairs of eyes along with satyrs and maenads. The figural decoration on the inner rim is unusual. On one side the sons of Boreas, Kalais and Zetes, drive out the Harpies who robbed blind King Phineus of his food; on the other is Dionysos with his merry following. This bowl occupies a special place in Chalkidian vase painting (see page 101) and seems to have been influenced by the rich mythological repertory of Attic products. Yet none of the other pottery workshops could match what Athens produced in this field, and only there did this class of pottery decoration have a future.

Around 525 B.C., the inhabitants of the island of Siphnos erected a treasury in Delphi (for its use, see page 117). The whole building was encircled by a relief frieze which represented the Battle before Troy, the Battle of the Gods and Giants, the Judgment of Paris, and the Rape of the Daughters of Leukippos. Two female figures (caryatids) carried the entablature on the entrance side, where Herakles and Apollo fighting for the tripod (see page 66) could be seen in the pediment. This detail shows five gods and goddesses on the side of the Trojans watching the battle: Ares, Aphrodite, Artemis, Apollo, and Zeus (who is seated on a splendid throne, the armrest of which is supported by the figures of a satyr and a maenad). On the right side of the east frieze appear the gods favorable to the Greeks. The relief friezes of the Treasury of the Siphnians are an outstanding example of Ionic art, whose serenity constituted an essential ingredient of Archaic art. Its influence on Attic art was also decisive, particularly in the elegance of the kore statues (see page 114). The signatures of Ionian artists on surviving pedestals prove that they, like other artists, were strongly attracted by the brilliance of Athens under the Peisistratid tyranny. Delight in exterior beauty, pleasing form, and variety of color, as well as a tendency to affected gestures and seemingly studied bearing, assured Ionic art of great success in Athens. Yet it was probably just this which aroused the opposition of those Attic artists who were to bring about the great break with Archaic art (see pages 126 ff.).

Council of the Gods. Marble with traces of red paint on a blue background, height 24³/₄″. Ionic, shortly before 525 B.C. From the east frieze of the Treasury of the Siphnians in Delphi. Museum, Delphi

Kore. Painted marble, height 71⁵⁄₈″. Attic, c. 520 B.C. From the Acropolis, Athens. Acropolis Museum, Athens

The statues of maidens (see page 109), particularly of Late Archaic times, which were found in great number principally on the Athenian Acropolis, are known as korai. They are votive offerings to Athena from the time of the tyrant Peisistratos (560–527 B.C.) and his sons. Like the kouros (see page 89), the kore is a fixed standard type. Here, the clothing consists of a chiton and a short cloak, which falls diagonally in fine folds. Her smiling expression (see page 97) adds to the effect produced by the aristocratic bearing of the figure.

The singular expression of the kore head on the facing page makes it one of the loveliest of its kind, although the holes to which the missing metal hairpiece was attached impair the effect to some extent.

Head of a Kore. Marble with traces of red and black paint (metal ornaments were fastened in the drill holes), height 5⁵⁄₈″. Attic, c. 510 B.C. From the Acropolis, Athens. Acropolis Museum, Athens

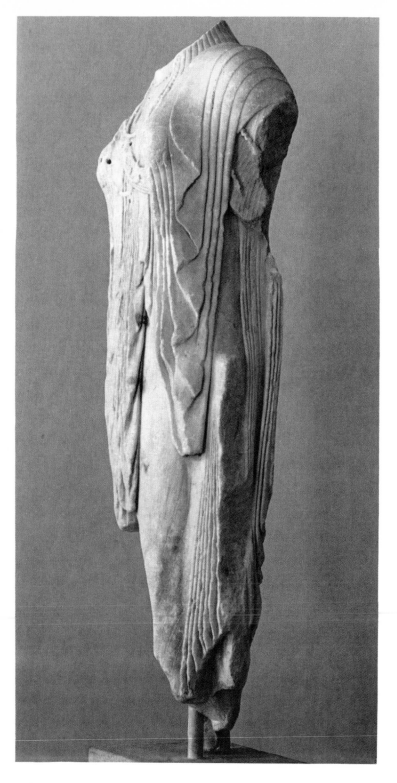

Kore. Marble, height 56¼". Cycladic, c. 510 B.C. From Delos. National Museum, Athens

The drapery of the garment of this figure, whose bearing corresponds to the kore type, is almost excessively ornate, and the artist seems to have lost himself in playful details. A kore of very similar style found on the Athenian Acropolis would seem to indicate that the artist who made this Delian example was also active in Athens (see page 114).

Treasury of the Athenians in Delphi. Marble, height 24′ 11″, length 31′ 9³/₄″, width 21′ 8¹/₂″. Attic, end of sixth century B.C. (rebuilt in 1906)

The Athenian Treasury has the form of a temple with two columns *in antis* (that is, set between the pilaster-like ends [*antae*] of the side walls to form a front colonnade). A Doric frieze with thirty metope reliefs representing the deeds of Herakles and Theseus runs right round the building. Cities which had given especially large quantities of costly votive offerings built treasuries in order to protect their donations. They and the temples provide the architectural accent within the walled sanctuary with its cult monuments, freestanding votive offerings, and statues. The Athenian Treasury in Delphi is the only one to have been successfully reconstructed, although plentiful remains of others have been found (see page 113).

A horseman, next to whom is inscribed the name Leagros, has been painted on the coral-red ground of the inside of this cup (right). On the outside are depicted the slaying of Geryon by Herakles and this three-bodied monster's great herd of cattle. The signatures of the potter Kachrylion and the painter Euphronios appear on the rim of the foot. Leagros gives us an idea of what an aristocratic Athenian youth of Late Archaic times must have looked like. He corresponds to a number of statues of horsemen from the Acropolis (below), early examples of a type which was to become popular as an important form of memorial statue.

Leagros. Cup (kylix) by Euphronios and Kachrylion. Terra cotta with glaze paint, diameter of cup 16⁷/₈″. Attic, c. 510 B.C. From Vulci (Etruria). Antikensammlung, Munich

◀ *Horse and Rider*. Marble painted brown, blue, and black, height 44″, length 31″. Attic, c. 510 B.C. From the Acropolis, Athens. Acropolis Museum, Athens

The picture, on the facing page, of the ▶ mythological wrestling match between Peleus and Thetis retains none of the original mystery of the tale. The attempt of Thetis to escape from Peleus' hold by changing into animal form is indicated only by the inclusion of a lion and snakes in the scene. The fight itself has more of the appearance of a posed dance movement.

Peleus Wrestling with Thetis. Cup (kylix) by Pei- ▶ thinos. Terra cotta with glaze paint, height 5¹/₈″, diameter 13³/₈″. Attic, shortly before 500 B.C. From Vulci (Etruria). State Museums, Berlin

Temple of Aphaia. Limestone coated with stucco and painted, c. 45 × 95′. Aeginetan, c. 500 B.C. On the northeast point of the island of Aegina

This Doric temple (see page 96) has six columns on the short sides and twelve on the long. The colonnade surrounds the temple proper, which consists of a three-aisled cella, or sanctuary, with a porch at either end, each of which has two columns *in antis* (see page 117). The temple was dedicated to the probably pre-Greek goddess Aphaia, whose name is known to us only through an inscription. In the pediments were marble sculptures (now in Munich) depicting scenes of the Trojan War. No trace has remained of the metopes: they may have been of wood and painted. The pediments were each crowned by a palmette tree flanked by two female figures, and at the corners were griffins. The magnificent effect of this richly decorated temple was further enlivened by color, for not only were the marble figures painted, but parts of the architecture as well. A fine white stucco covered the limestone, while the decorative members of the structure were accented in red and blue and only the columns and the architraves remained completely white.

Man Hurrying to the Aid of a Fallen Warrior (detail). Marble, over-all height of the figure 38″. Aeginetan, c. 490 B.C. From the right half of the east pediment of the temple of Aphaia at Aegina. (The restored nose has now been removed.) Glyptothek, Munich

As important examples of Aeginetan art, the pediment sculptures of the temple of Aphaia still manifest a strong bond with Archaic form. This is surprising, since the Aeginetan artist of this period was later considered to be a great pioneer. (Compare the hairstyle with that on page 142.)

The departure of Triptolemos, sent by Demeter to bring agriculture to mankind, is painted round the steep walls of this drinking cup. The youthful Triptolemos sits on his serpent-chariot; Persephone pours him a libation; Demeter looks on from behind. The sheaves of wheat which Triptolemos and Demeter hold in their hands allude to the god's mission. The others present—Zeus, Poseidon, Dionysos, Amphitrite, as well as Eleusis and Eumolpos—are identified by inscriptions. Hieron's signature is incised into one of the handles. The red-figure technique, in which the figures are reserved so that they stand out from the shiny deep-black of the glaze paint, can here be seen in all its beauty. The sharp contrast of light and dark, not the least impaired by the sparingly used purple color (for details and inscriptions), is in tune with the general rejection of the colorfulness of Archaic art. This was manifested in the old black-figure vase painting (see pages 84, 86, 101) by the rich use of red and white color on the black silhouettes of the figures, as well as in the ornamental motifs scattered over the background. The inner drawing, which was formerly scratched into the dark glaze paint with a needle and appeared light, is now executed in black as a "relief line." The treacly consistency of the glaze paint makes the line drawn with a fine brush stand out in relief on the ground and catch the light.

Skyphos, by Hieron (potter) and Makron (painter). Terra cotta with glaze paint, height 8¼". Attic, c. 485 B.C. From Capua (southern Italy). British Museum, London

White-ground lekythos. Terra cotta with cream-colored slip and glaze paint, white color for the skin, height 14¾". Attic, c. 490 B.C. The Hermitage, Leningrad

This exceptionally fine picture of the goddess Artemis feeding a swan has been recognized as the work of the Pan Painter. The Archaic delicacy and precision in the long folds of the garment are given a final and intentional exaggeration, making the whole seem "Archaistic." The white-ground lekythoi, in which the ground of the picture zone is covered with a white slip (coating of liquid clay), form an essential part of Attic funeral furnishings (see pages 167, 168). They were containers for oil, given to the dead for use in the afterlife. The great amount of oil used for this purpose—and thus withdrawn from the national economy—forced the authorities to regulate the maximum quantities permissible. For this reason, some of the lekythoi have an insert which made the jar seem full even when it contained only a small amount of oil. Their particular form set high demands on the potter's art.

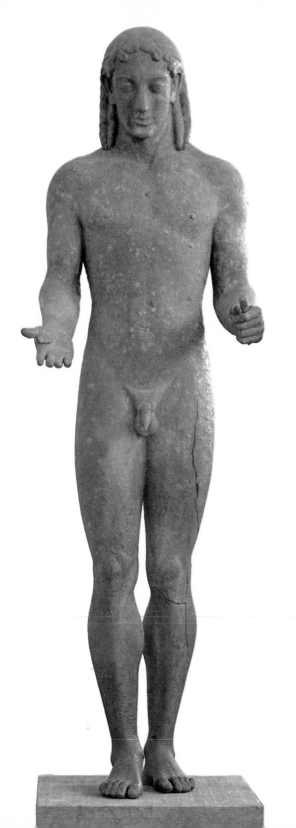

Standing Youth. Bronze, height 75⅝″. Attic, c. 480 B.C. (?) From Piraeus. National Museum, Athens

At first sight, this youth looks like an Archaic kouros (see page 89), but the flowing sculptural forms, the right foot set forward, the inclination and turn of the head, are un-Archaic features. Nor had Archaic art produced any life-sized bronze statues up to this point. The youth held a bowl in his right hand and some slender object (a bow?) in his left: he may be the god Apollo. The statue appears to be the work of an artistically conservative master.

This standing woman, identified by the dove in her right hand and by the Erotes as Aphrodite, wears a simple peplos, corresponding to fifth-century B.C. fashion; but she gathers it up with her left hand like the Archaic korai. She thus exemplifies the long survival of the Archaic element, above all in the minor arts. The volute ornament growing from the head of the goddess held the round mirror, which was supported at the back by a palmette.

Aphrodite and Erotes. Support for a mirror. Bronze, height 6¼″. 480–460 B.C. From Sounion. British Museum, London

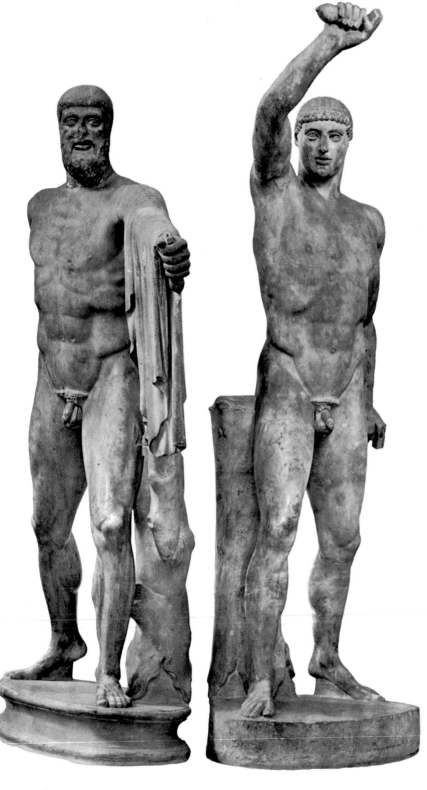

The Tyrannicides (Harmodios and Aristogeiton). Marble, height 76³/₄″. Roman copies of bronze originals by Kritios and Nesiotes, 477–476 B.C. From Rome. Museo Nazionale, Naples

Beneath this group, which shows only the two conspirators and not their victim, ran the inscription: "A great light fell upon the Athenians, for Aristogeiton together with Harmodios slew Hipparchos ... [and freed thereby] the land of our fathers." The two tyrannicides, who in 514 B.C. slew Hipparchos, son of Peisistratos, and prepared the way for Athenian democracy, were probably honored soon afterward by the erection of statues. The first group by Antenor was carried off to Persia in 480 B.C. by Xerxes. In 477 B.C., victorious Athens renewed the monument, and the copies which have survived reproduce this second work by Kritios and Nesiotes. The group was a symbol of the Greek love of freedom and a warning to all those who dared attack the democratic form of government.

THE FIFTH CENTURY B.C.

The fall of the tyrants of Athens in 510 B.C., the establishment of the democracy—that is, the transferral of power from the state represented by an individual to the masses—and the Persian Wars mark the period which divides Archaic art from that of the fifth century B.C. The first victory over the Persians at Marathon (490 B.C.) proved the superiority of the new political structure of the state. Despite the destruction of Athens by the Persians (480 B.C.), this mighty foe from the East was defeated both at sea (Salamis, 480 B.C.) and on land (Plataia, 479 B.C.), and was driven from Greek soil. This victory proved the validity of the new ideas and forms the background for the magnificent flowering of Greek genius in all fields during the fifth century B.C. The devastation wreaked by the Persians necessitated new building; the summit of the Acropolis could now be leveled and new temple structures planned (see page 128). The economic upsurge of Athens was the basis of the realization of the many daring projects which made this city the great political and cultural center of Greece. The Greek scene now changed and the remaining regions lost that artistic independence which had made Archaic art so varied. This concentration alone made possible the breakthrough in art which not only opened the way to the future but also resulted in a consciousness of the fact that it was uniquely "classic." We do not use this term today in the sense of something exemplary and worthy of imitation; however, the admiration which its contemporaries probably, and later generations certainly, accorded the art of the fifth century B.C. (and which is historically justified) is well expressed in the concept of "classicism."

This statue (the so-called *Kritios Boy*) for the first time represents a human being resting his weight on one leg (see page 162). This relaxed posture resulted in a new distribution of weight which led to technical difficulties in marble statues. For this reason artists preferred to work in bronze.

Standing Boy. Marble, height 33⅞". Before 480 B.C. From the Acropolis, Athens. Acropolis Museum, Athens

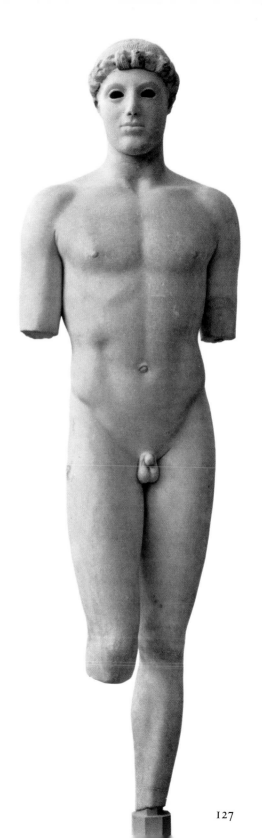

The Acropolis of Athens. View from the southwest, from the Monument of Philopappos

After its devastation by the Persians in 480 B.C., the Acropolis of Athens, which had been a citadel ever since Mycenaean times, was fortified by new walls under Kimon and Perikles and decorated with the magnificent buildings which still today determine its outline. The mighty structure of the Parthenon (see page 150) rose up over the plateau, and next to it the Erechtheion (see page 166) appeared small and delicate. Further west is the Propylaia (see page 156) and, on the bastions in front of this, the temple of Athena Nike (see page 170). On the south slope of the rock rises the façade of the Odeion which Herodes Atticus had built shortly after A.D. 161. This was connected by the stoa (whose rear wall still stands) of Eumenes II of Pergamon (197–159 B.C., see page 250) with the old theater of Dionysos (see page 169), the auditorium of which, sunk into the rock, can be seen in the photograph.

The statuette of a young athlete (two views of which are reproduced on the facing page) shows the flexible body turning freely and leaning back to counterbalance the weight of the (now missing) discus in his right hand. It may be a copy of a large-scale statue, for it was through such difficult subjects as this that sculptors could now best reveal the motion which had long been fettered by Archaic rules. Myron (see page 146) and Pythagoras were the leading artists in this field (see also page 136).

Discus Thrower. Bronze statuette, height $7^7/_8''$. 480–470 B.C. From the Acropolis, Athens. National Museum, Athens

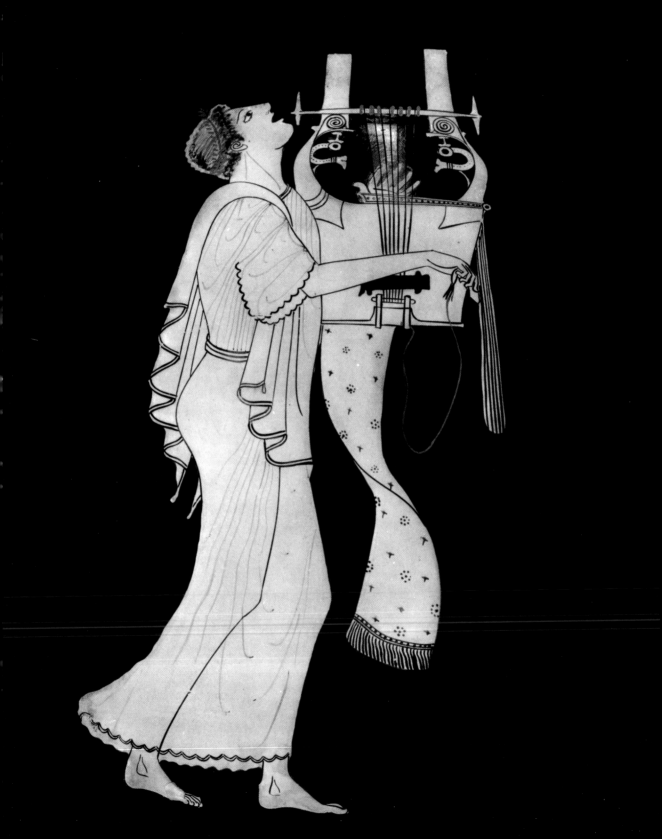

Kithara Player. Detail of an amphora. Terra cotta with glaze paint, height of the figure 8½". Attic, c. 480 B.C. From Nola (southern Italy). The Metropolitan Museum of Art, New York

Herakles, Atlas, and Athena. Metope from the temple of Zeus at Olympia. Marble, height 63". c. 460 B.C. Museum, Olympia

The twelve metopes of the temple of Zeus represent the twelve labors of Herakles; the east pediment showed the preparation for the chariot race between Pelops and Oinomaos; and the west pediment the battle of Lapiths and centaurs (see page 134). The great temple (c. 217 feet long) by the architect Libon housed Pheidias' gold and ivory statue of Zeus (see page 155). The Atlas metope shows Herakles supporting the heavenly vault, which, understood to be outside the actual relief, weighs down on him. A cushion and, above all, the helping hand of the goddess Athena make the weight bearable. In return for his help, Atlas brings him the apples of the Hesperides.

This graceful figure of a kithara player by the Pan Painter lends expression to the magic of music. What cannot be represented—the music itself—is indicated by the effect that it has on the player. On the reverse, the presiding judge of a competition is shown.

Herakles Cleaning the Augean Stables. Metope from the temple of Zeus at Olympia. Marble, height 63". c. 460 B.C. Museum, Olympia ▶

Head of Athena. Fragment of a metope from the temple of Zeus at Olympia. Marble, height 9⅞". c. 460 B.C. Museum, Olympia

Athena looked down toward her protégé Herakles who, exhausted by his adventure, rested his foot upon the slain Nemean lion. The hair above her left eye, which could not be seen when the sculpture was in its original position, was indicated by paint. The art of Olympia, as it appears in the pediment figures and metopes of the temple of Zeus, is anonymous. We have just as little reliable information about the origins of the architect Libon as we do about the pediment sculptors. It is certain, however, that the influence of Attic art and probably also of contemporary large-scale painting can be felt in the sculptural decoration of the temple.

Herakles uses his own great strength to cleanse the neglected stables of King Augias of Elis (facing page). In the classic version of the story, he diverted the rushing torrents of a river to accomplish the task. Athena, here with shield and helmet, supports him by her presence.

Battle of Lapiths and Centaurs. Frieze on the neck of a volute krater. Terra cotta with glaze paint, over-all height of the vase 25″, of the frieze c. 4″. c. 450 B.C. From Italy. The Metropolitan Museum of Art, New York

Both the picture of a battle with Amazons on the body of the vessel and that of a centauromachy (above) reveal the influence of large-scale painting, which—according to the evidence of numerous literary sources—made use of both subjects.

The battle between the Lapiths (a people of Thessaly) and the centaurs (see page 68) occurred at the wedding feast of Peirithoös, a friend of Theseus, to which the centaurs had been invited. Intoxicated with wine, they laid hands on the maidens and youths present. The resulting fight, in which every kind of improvised weapon was used, was one of the favorite subjects of Greek art (see pages 152, 165). Together with the Amazonomachy, in which Herakles, Achilles, or Theseus is the leader of the Greeks (see pages 135, 140, 154, 200), and the battle of the gods and giants, the battle with the centaurs is a symbol of the desire of the Greeks for self-assertion. The theme therefore appeared with great frequency in the art of the fifth century B.C. after the victory of Greece over Persia.

West (top) and east pediments of the temple of Zeus at Olympia. c. 460 B.C. Reconstruction drawings

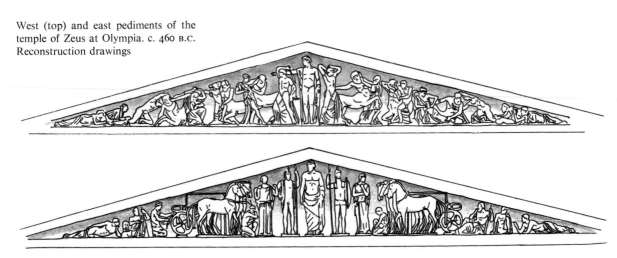

Battle of Greeks and Amazons. Calyx krater. Terra cotta with glaze paint, height 22″. c. 460–450 B.C. From Italy. The Metropolitan Museum of Art, New York

The front and back of this krater are decorated with a continuous picture of a battle of Greeks and Amazons. The pains which the artist took in his perspective rendering of the mounted Amazon in the center can give us only a vague idea of the work of a great painter such as Kimon or Polygnotos. Their masterly achievements in this field are unfortunately only known to us through later literary references. Vase paintings such as this (see also page 136) illustrate the limitations of this art form: from now on, vase painting and large-scale painting are considered specific classes of art, and the former becomes a "minor art."

Youth with a Horse. Fragment of
a cup by the potter Kachrylion.
Terra cotta with glaze paint,
diameter 2³/₄". c. 480 B.C. From
Gela, Sicily. Museo Nazionale,
Syracuse

Pegasus. Coin (trihemiobol). Silver, height
³/₈", length ¹/₂". From Corinth. L. Milden-
berg Collection.

A famous painting by Polygnotos in
Delphi showed a laden donkey seen
from the front and a horse rolling on
the ground. The minor arts also at-
tempted to adopt such innovations.

Head of a Woman. Marble relief, height 12³/₄″, width 13¹/₈″ (diameter originally c. 18″). Parian, c. 460 B.C. From Melos. National Museum, Athens

This head has been variously identified as a representation of Aphrodite, of a local nymph, and of the moon-goddess Selene. However, this last would have occupied only about half of the original circle and can therefore be ruled out. It may be that the missing part of the relief contained an identifying inscription. Today, both the question of her identity and of whether this was a votive relief or part of a tombstone remain unanswered.

Simple yet impressive, this head is an example of Ionic art, adding a special sensitivity to the sobriety of contemporary Attic heads.

The front and reverse sides of this drinking cup make up a single scene: below, Odysseus lets fly his arrows; on the facing page, they strike the surprised carousing suitors of Penelope. Frightened maidservants look on in amazement. In the temple of Athena Areia in Plataia, Polygnotos had painted Odysseus "after he had slain the suitors," and therefore not as dramatically as the painter of this skyphos. On another skyphos in Chiusi (Italy), the same artist (known as the Penelope Painter) represented Penelope at her loom with Telemachos,

Odysseus Slaying the Suitors. Skyphos. Terra cotta with glaze paint, height 7³/₄″. Attic, c. 450 B.C. From Tarquinia. State Museums, Berlin

and the foot-washing scene in which the old nurse recognizes her returning master by a scar. The influence of large-scale painting is evident in both, even though many painters, particularly Polygnotos, had given up the "narrative" style in favor of the "situation" picture. Polygnotos' Odysseus was probably similar to the Herakles in the lion metope from Olympia (a fragment of which is reproduced on page 132), sunk in thought after the death of the suitors.

This scene of an Amazonomachy depicts the moment in which Achilles kills the Queen of the Amazons, Penthesileia, and—too late—recognizes that they love each other. In its use of color and in the way in which the
figures burst through the limits of the picture zone, it is an example of the attempt made by the vase painter to
keep in step with large-scale painting. Mikon painted a battle of Greeks and Amazons twice, and it may be
that a reflection of one of these works has been caught in this picture. The psychological moment shown is
characteristic of the painting of the time.

The Athenian sculptors of the Olympia metopes (see pages 131–33) had already "humanized" their gods, ▶
the result of the new attitude of the Greeks to their divinities. The votive relief on the facing page shows Athena
dressed in a simple peplos, her only armor a helmet. She leans on her spear and looks down at a pillar, which
may be a boundary stone, a stele inscribed with a legal edict, a temple inventory, or perhaps the winning post
of a palaestra. The actual content of the art works of this period is not always as easy to grasp as in older
examples. The ethos, the mood, permeates the entire scene, inviting meditation in the observer.

Death of Penthesileia. Kylix. Terra cotta with glaze paint and much use of color and gilded relief, diameter of the bowl 16⁷/₈″. Attic, c. 460 B.C. From Vulci. Antikensammlung, Munich

"Mourning Athena." Marble relief, height 21¹/₄″. c. 455 B.C. From the Acropolis of Athens. Acropolis Museum, Athens

This statue, one of the few original bronze masterpieces to have escaped destruction, is complete except for the trident, which the god was in the act of hurling, and the eyes, which were once inlaid with colored materials. Every attempt to identify this work with a specific statue mentioned in literary sources or to attribute it to one or another famous master on stylistic grounds has so far failed. Poseidon wears the braided coiffure usual for the time (see page 121). Despite his completely human aspect, the god differs from an athlete in the deliberate calm which emanates from the entire figure, and particularly from the face.

The statue below probably represented Agon, the personification of competition. The giving of form to abstract ideas was one of the new tasks which the visual arts set themselves in the first half of the fifth century B.C. The challenging turn of the head would be consistent with such an explanation. Competition is a concept which took on special meaning in the fifth century B.C., for not only was athletic prowess measured in Olympia, Delphi, and Isthmia, but Agon also ruled over poetry and the visual arts. Contests between sculptors (see pages 159, 172) were just as natural as those between dramatists and musicians (see page 207).

Poseidon. Bronze, height 82¹/₄". c. 455 B.C. Found in the sea off Cape Artemision on the north coast of Euboea. National Museum, Athens

Head of a Youth. Copy of an original of c. 460 B.C. Marble, over-all height of the statue 62¹/₂". From Greece (?). The Hermitage, Leningrad

Athena, from the group of *Athena and Marsyas.* Roman copy of the bronze original by Myron on the Acropolis of Athens. Marble, height 68$\frac{1}{8}$". Original c. 450 B.C. From Via Gregoriano (Pincio), Rome. Liebieghaus, Frankfurt

Pausanias saw this group on the Acropolis and wrote (I, 24, 1) that here was "Athena, striking Marsyas Silenus for taking up the flutes that the goddess wished to be cast away for good"; and we learn the name of the master from Pliny (34, 57): "Myron made a satyr, admiring the flutes, and Athena." Neither of these descriptions is, in fact, completely accurate, for Athena does not strike Marsyas, and it is something more than admiration that determines Marsyas' movement. He wants to snatch up the pipes that Athena has thrown away, while the goddess looks at him with disdain; for, unlike herself, the fact that flute playing distorts the face would not bother him in the least. Copies of the figure of Marsyas have also survived, so that a reconstruction of the group is possible (see opposite). Only the position of the spear and the gesture of Athena's left hand are uncertain.

Athena and Marsyas, by Myron. Bronze reconstruction in the original size. National Museum, Warsaw, formerly in the Städtisches Museum, Stettin

Discus Thrower. Roman copy of the bronze statue by Myron. Marble, height 60¹/₄". Original c. 450 B.C. Museo Nazionale, Rome

Myron was one of the most important artists to represent moving figures in free-standing sculpture. His running *Ladas,* as well as the *Discus Thrower,* of which several copies have survived, were famous. Without the support, the bronze original must have conveyed the swing of the athletic body even more convincingly. After this "classical" solution, no further attempts were made to surpass it. Here is one of the finest examples of an artist's choice of the "pregnant moment." It is this brief pause, at the highest point of the upswing of the arm, just before the downward swing which will hurl the discus into the distance, that Myron recognized as the most characteristic instant in the complicated process of discus throwing.

In the illustration on the facing page, the vase painter has succeeded as almost never before in capturing something of the powerful effect of panel painting in his technically more modest work. A breathless calm floats over this picture of the return of Persephone from the depths of the earth. Hekate, who illuminates the scene with her torches, seems to call her forth by magic; Hermes stands nearby as escort; while Demeter (off the picture, to the right) looks impassively upon her long-sought daughter. The whole painting expresses a feeling of deliverance after a long and desperate wait.

The secret mystery cults of Eleusis which, in the fifth century B.C., had an important place alongside the cult of the Olympian gods—and into which the leading men of the time were initiated—are based on belief in this resurrection. The powerful effect of these mysteries becomes more comprehensible in the presence of such a picture. On the reverse of the vase an offering scene is represented.

Persephone Returning from the Underworld. Detail of a calyx krater. Terra cotta with glaze paint, height of the vessel 16$\frac{1}{8}$″, of the scene 7$\frac{7}{8}$″. Attic, c. 440 B.C. The Metropolitan Museum of Art, New York

The reclining god, still unaware of the great event which is taking place behind him in the center of the pediment—the birth of the goddess Athena from the head of Zeus—looks toward the rising quadriga of Helios in the left corner of the pediment. The figure fitted into the triangular form of the pediment (see the cast on page 150), which consistently set particular problems for the artist (see also page 134). Any impression of spatial restriction has been avoided with great mastery, and the reclining form is developed freely and naturally within its allotted space. Even without divine attributes, the superhuman quality of the god can be recognized in the majestic calm of his appearance.

Dionysos. Marble, height 47^1/$_2$". c. 437–432 B.C. From the east pediment of the Parthenon, Athens. British Museum, London

Head of a Horse of Selene's Quadriga. Marble, length 33⁷/₈″. c. 437–432 B.C. From the east pediment of the Parthenon, Athens. British Museum, London

This horse's head, whose mouth projected over the edge of the pediment, belongs to the team of the moon-goddess, going down in the right corner of the pediment. She and the rising sun-god framed the central scene, the birth of Athena. Goethe observed that the sculptor of the horse's head had "really made a primeval horse, whether he had actually seen it with his eyes, or merely imagined it; at least to us it seems to have been represented in accordance with the greatest poetry and reality."

Here, in the east pediment of the Parthenon, is the first occurrence of an event framed by Helios and Selene. The scene is thus set in a place in time which, on the one hand, warns of the transitoriness of time and, on the other, emphasizes the uniqueness of the event.

The Parthenon (east façade), by the architects Iktinos and Kallikrates. Pentelic marble, c. 228 × 101′. 447–438 B.C. On the Acropolis of Athens

The temple of Athena Parthenos was the heart of the Acropolis (see page 128) and of Athens as a whole. The magnificent structure of Periklean times is entirely of marble, with eight columns along the front, seventeen at the sides, and inner porticoes of six columns each. The cella is three-aisled, the roof of the adyton (inner sanctuary) was supported by four columns. The pediments contained scenes of the birth of Athena (see pages 148, 149) and of the contest between Athena and Poseidon for the ownership of Attica. Ninety-two metopes illustrated battles of centaurs (see page 152), of Amazons, of gods and giants, and of Greeks and Trojans. A frieze, some 525 feet long, was carved on the outside of the inner building, immortalizing the Panathenaic procession (see facing page).

It is evident that, over and above its religious function, the Parthenon was intended to display the might and culture of Athens to the whole world. In wonder, Plutarch (A.D. 45–125) wrote about the buildings of Perikles (*Per.* 13): "A youthful freshness hovers over these works, preserving their aspect untouched by time, as though they had had breathed into them an aura of youthfulness and a strength to render them imperishable." This impression is partly due to the fact that there is not a single mathematically straight line, which would have been considered too cold and dead, in the whole building. The "curvature" of the stylobate (see page 96) amounted to $2^3/_8''$ on the short axis and $4^3/_8''$ on the long, and was continued in the superstructure. Pheidias supervised the sculptures of the Acropolis and also made the gold and ivory image of Athena Parthenos (see page 153).

The fragment of the east frieze of the Parthenon in the Louvre shows a group of girls at the head of the Panathenaic procession. They march from the north toward the center of the east frieze, where the new peplos woven by the Athenian maidens is handed over to the goddess. Here also are two groups of seated gods awaiting the arrival of the procession—loosely arranged on the west, but regularly organized on the north and south —as it approaches the east front.

The solemn calm, the controlled movement, and the restrained low relief are so timeless that the concept of "classic" seems to be summed up in this frieze, which was originally barely visible high up on the cella wall.

Girls and Festival Organizers. Fragment of the east frieze of the Parthenon, Athens. Marble, height $41^3/_8''$. c. 440 B.C. The Louvre, Paris

Centauromachy. Metope from the south side of the Parthenon, Athens. Marble, height 52³/₄″. 447–442 B.C. British Museum, London

On the south side of the Parthenon, to the right and left of a central group of nine metopes whose significance has not yet been convincingly explained, were twenty-three others with variations on the old theme of fighting centaurs. Some of these metopes seem older, rather wooden, in their movement, others looser and full of power, while still others emphasize the beauty of the human body by means of impressive poses and rhythmic draping of the garments.

It is to be assumed that the thirty-two metopes are all related in content. Thus, since the nine in the center have so far evaded all attempts at explanation, the centaur battle here represented cannot be positively identified with any of those so far known (see page 134). It may illustrate a local Attic legend.

Athena Parthenos. Copy of the gold and ivory cult statue by Pheidias in the Parthenon, Athens. Marble, height 41³/₈″. Original completed c. 438 B.C. From Athens. National Museum, Athens

This statuette of Athena Parthenos only partially reproduces the wealth of figural decoration that Pausanias describes so precisely (see also page 248). The gigantic cult image of the patron goddess of Athens in the main temple on the Periklean Acropolis (see page 150) was the work of Pheidias. It was of gold and ivory and must have stood almost forty feet high. The gold, said to have weighed over a ton and comprising a goodly portion of the state treasure, was detachable, so that its weight could be checked at any time. The helmet of the goddess bore a sphinx and two griffins; the shield had an Amazonomachy (Amazon battle) on the outside and a gigantomachy (battle of gods and giants) on the inside; and a centauromachy was depicted on the edges of her sandals. On the base of the statue was a relief of the birth of Pandora framed, like the birth of Athena on the east pediment of the temple (see page 149), by Helios and Selene. The goddess stood in a frontal position and held in her right hand a Nike, who seemed relatively small despite the fact that she was over five feet high. This cult statue and that of Zeus in Olympia (see page 155) brought Pheidias—primarily a sculptor of the gods —particular fame.

Amazon Leaping to Her Death. Copy in the original size of a group on the shield of the *Athena Parthenos* by Pheidias. Marble, 36¼ × 50¾″. From Piraeus. Archaeological Museum, Piraeus

Pheidias decorated the shield of his *Athena Parthenos* with scenes of Amazon battles, which were often copied. Framed replicas of details, which sank in the harbor of Piraeus as they were about to be sent to Rome, include two scenes which also appear on a marble reproduction of the shield in London. Here, an Amazon hurls herself into space in her effort to escape.

Zeus, by Pheidias. Representations of the head and of the whole figure on Hadrianic coins. State Museums, Berlin; Archaeological Museum, Florence

Pheidias' masterpiece, the forty-foot high cult image in the temple of Zeus in Olympia, is mentioned by Pausanias and highly praised by many other writers. Since no copies exist, we must rely on reproductions on coins for an over-all impression of the statue.

Copies of the reliefs on the god's throne have been identified in marble sculptures depicting the slaying of the children of Niobe. These can be reconstructed into two friezes (one on each of the armrests), in which Apollo kills Niobe's sons and Artemis her daughters.

Pheidias may have made this figure after his enforced flight from Athens in 438 B.C.

The Slaying of the Children of Niobe. Reconstruction of reliefs on the throne of the statue of Zeus by Pheidias

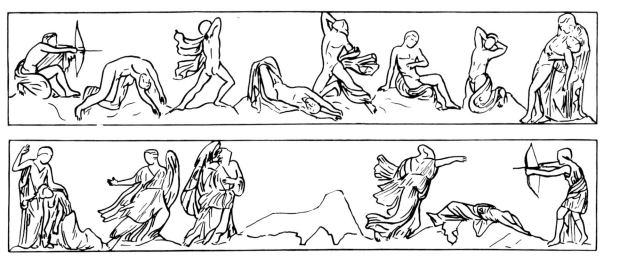

The Propylaia, by the architect Mnesikles. Marble. 438–432 B.C. On the Acropolis of Athens

Perikles intended that the temples of the Acropolis should not gradually appear to the visitor as he climbed the hill, but that, by stepping through a monumental portal, he should find himself suddenly confronted by them (see page 128). This splendid ascent to the Acropolis was, however, never achieved, for the south wing of the gate building remained unfinished. The columns of the façade, six on each side, are Doric. The three on either side of the passageway are Ionic. The Propylaia, a secular building, and the temple of the goddess Athena are lasting symbols of that golden age that Athens experienced under the leadership of Perikles (460–429 B.C.).

Temple of Athena and Hephaistos (so-called Theseion). Marble, 45 × 104'. 450–440 B.C. On the western edge of the Athenian Agora

This temple—the best-preserved in Greece—overlooks the market place in the lower city of Athens. It dates from about the same time as the Parthenon. The east front is decorated with metopes depicting the labors of Herakles and Theseus (hence "Theseion"); but only the ten metopes over the entrance and the four adjoining at each side have relief carvings. Of the pediment decorations nothing but fragments have survived. The temple towers over the Agora, the secular center of the city, whose installations were destroyed by the Persian invaders in 480 B.C.

The goddess wears a peplos and an aegis, which crosses her body diagonally like a sash. She held her helmet in her right hand. Pheidias' *Athena Lemnia* was famous for her great beauty and was probably dedicated by Athenian citizens who moved to Lemnos. Pausanias (I, 28, 2), Pliny (34,54), and other writers used words of the highest praise in mentioning her. In contrast to the awe-inspiring might of Pheidias' *Athena Parthenos* (see page 153), her benevolence toward the Athenians is emphasized here by the same sculptor in an interpretation almost as human as that embodied at its loveliest in the votive relief from the Acropolis (see page 141).

Athena. Copy of bronze original, probably the *Athena Lemnia* made by Pheidias for the Athenian Acropolis. Marble, height $81^1/_2$". c. 445 B.C. Staatliche Kunstsammlungen, Dresden

Leaning on her spear, the wounded Amazon—identified by a spur strap as a horsewoman—drags herself from the battlefield. The statue was the result of a competition in which Pheidias, Polykleitos, Kresilas, and Phradmon took part. Pheidias only received second prize. The original statues stood in the sanctuary of Artemis in Ephesos, and copies of all four were apparently set up in Hadrian's Villa.

Amazon, by Pheidias. Copy of bronze original in Ephesos. Marble, height (without base) 86″. Original c. 430 B.C. From Hadrian's Villa, near Tivoli. Antiquarium, Hadrian's Villa, Tivoli

Polykleitos of Argos, a master in the depiction of the human body, but said to have been surpassed by Pheidias in the representation of gods, carried off the laurels in the Amazon competition. His wounded Amazon has reached the sanctuary of Artemis and supports herself on a post. Polykleitos later repeated this innovation (in which, for the first time, a part of the weight of the body is shifted to an object next to the figure) in other statues. It was probably this surprising solution which brought Polykleitos first prize (Pliny, 34, 53; see page 159).

Amazon, by Polykleitos. Copy of bronze original in Ephesos. Marble, height 80¹/₄″. Original c. 430 B.C. The Metropolitan Museum of Art, New York

The Amazon wears a riding cloak and leans on her spear in Polykleitan fashion —a lack of innovation that brought the statue only third prize. Kresilas' fame was based primarily on his portrait statues, of which that of Perikles was particularly famous. The name Sosikles incised on the support next to the leg of the Amazon is presumably that of the copyist.

Amazon, by Kresilas. Copy of bronze original in Ephesos. Marble, height 79$^1/_2$". Original c. 430 B.C. Capitoline Museum, Rome

Doryphoros (Spear Bearer), by Polykleitos. Copy of bronze original. Marble, height 83¹/₂″. Original c. 440 B.C. From the palaestra at Pompeii. Museo Nazionale, Naples

The *Spear Bearer* was Polykleitos' best-known work and it seems probable that the sculptor created here a sort of "canonical" figure, just as he had also explained his art theoretically in a book. The copy from Pompeii is the best-preserved and only the spear in the left hand is missing. The right hand hangs down freely—for the first time in a statue.

This figure shows the characteristic walking pose, in which the weight of the body rests on one foot while the relaxed leg bears no weight. After the conquest of the Archaic kouros type (see pages 89, 90, 108, 110) and the preparatory transitional forms (see page 127) Polykleitos' "discovery" completely liberated the human form. The sloping line of the hips resulting from this pose is carried through the torso into a correspondingly opposed shoulder line (*contrapposto*), and all parts of the body are drawn into this movement.

Even in Antiquity the *Diadoumenos* seemed "softer" (Pliny 34, 35) when compared with the athletic figure of the *Doryphoros*. The walking pose is combined with a movement of the arms completely unlike that of the *Spear Bearer*.

The name "Diadoumenos" comes from the fact that, as victor of the competitions he founded, Theseus wears a fillet bound around his head. With the *Doryphoros,* it was the best-known work of Polykleitos, who probably executed this image of the Attic hero during his Athenian period.

Theseus Diadoumenos (detail), by Polykleitos. Copy of bronze original. Marble, over-all height, 72⁷/₈″. c. 440 B.C. The Metropolitan Museum of Art, New York

Temple of Apollo, Bassae (Triphylia), by the architect Iktinos.
Local dull-gray stone; the sculptural decoration, interior cap-
itals, and roof in marble; c. 47′ 6″ × 125′ 4″. c. 425–410 B.C.

According to Pausanias (VIII, 41, 9), this temple, set high up in the mountains, was built by Iktinos, one of the architects of the Parthenon. It is striking for its relative length (six columns by fifteen) as well as for the formation of the cella, inside which short projecting walls attached the engaged columns to the side walls. A relief frieze ran along the architrave. A single Corinthian column marked the dividing line between the adyton (inner sanctuary) and the cella proper. The metopes at the front and back of the cella were decorated with reliefs, but no trace of pediment figures has survived.

Even though the architect, perhaps in consideration of the local workmen and the hardness of the rock, gave the temple no curvature (see page 150), the unique spatial form of the cella marks him as an important and unconventional artist. Thus credence can be given the traditional attribution of the design to Iktinos.

The friezes of the temple were evidently executed by local artists. To the west and north of the inside of the cella were depicted battles of centaurs, while the east and south friezes represented Herakles' battle with the Amazons. In style, the reliefs reveal a certain conservatism together with an attempt to keep astride of the new art. Older motifs go hand in hand with the delight in flowing lines (see pages 171–75) characteristic of the end of the century. The "classic" form found in the Parthenon frieze (see page 151) is absent, for that could not be imitated.

Centauromachy and *Amazonomachy,* from the Temple of Apollo, Bassae. Marble, height 25^1/$_4$". c. 420–410 B.C. British Museum, London

The Erechtheion. Marble, height of the columns of the porch, 21′ 6″; height of the caryatids 7′ 9″. 420–406 B.C. On the Acropolis of Athens

White-ground lekythos. Terra cotta with white slip and mat painting in red and blue, height of detail c. 8″. c. 430 B.C. From Eretria. National Museum, Athens

The building of the Erechtheion probably began during that short period of peace (the Peace of Nikias, 421–415 B.C.) which briefly interrupted the Peloponnesian War (431–404 B.C.). In comparison with the austerity of the Parthenon (see page 150), this temple has something gay and delicate about it—a feeling that is provided not only by the slender Ionic columns (see page 128) but also by the multiplicity of its members and its rich ornamentation. The main decoration, the Caryatid Porch, returns to an Archaic motif (see page 113). The use of human figures as supports for the entablature is made new and pleasing in the clever rhythmical variations of the standard type of the maiden (kore). While dependence on Archaic models cannot be denied, the temple is not in itself an archaistic feature, but rather the expression of a strong reaction against the excessive restraint of the Periklean buildings and the beginning of a new joy in beauty of detail. The frieze, with its white marble figures against a darker ground and its exceedingly fine ornamentation animated by inlaid molten glass and gilded bronze bands and rosettes, emphasized the delicacy, the fineness, and perhaps even the playfulness of the building, in which the style of the third generation of the fifth century B.C. was completely embodied.

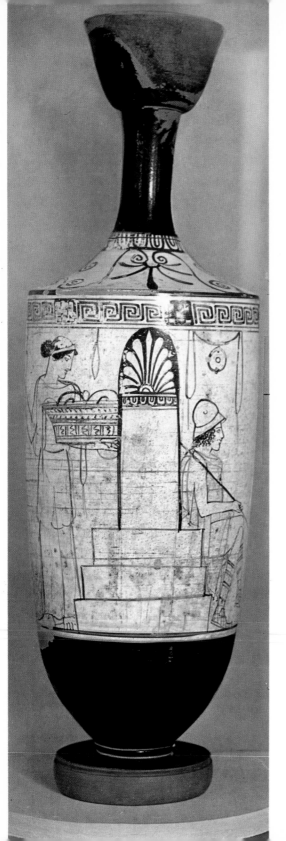

Fragment of an Attic white-ground lekythos. Terra cotta with white slip and red painting, height 4³/₄". c. 425–410 B.C. National Museum, Athens

White-ground lekythos. Terra cotta with white slip and golden-yellow paint, height c. 14". c. 450 B.C. From Eretria. National Museum, Athens

Theater of Dionysos on the south slope of the Athenian Acropolis, seen from above

This theater, in which the tragedies of Aischylos, Sophokles, and Euripides were presented, belongs to the sanctuary of Dionysos. In about 420 B.C., the stage and the orchestra, which had formerly been circular, were closed off from the rest of the sanctuary by a hall. The stepped seats follow the natural fall of the land (see page 128) and were faced with marble. The theater was in use until the end of Antiquity and was constantly transformed, its present design being largely the result of rebuilding in Roman times.

The white-ground lekythoi, some of which were painted with the usual glaze paint and some with gay mat colors, were for the use of the dead. The delicacy of execution and the expressions of the youth and girl on the fragment opposite (who were originally gazing at a tombstone in the center of the picture) provide an idea of the masterworks created by the painter Parrhasios of Ephesos. It was he who supplied Pheidias with the sketches for the centauromachy on the shield of *Athena Promachos* (Pausanias I, 28, 2) and whose drawings were particularly prized (Pliny 35, 68).

This small Ionic temple consists of a simple space open at the front (c. 18' 6" × 27') with engaged pilasters and with four columns at the front and back. The structure goes back to an older project by the Parthenon architect Kallikrates. The temple was demolished and its parts re-used, but it was later possible to re-erect it with the original building materials.

The Nike temple precinct was enclosed by a balustrade decorated on the outside with reliefs. Even in Antiquity the Nike who leans down to unlace her sandal (facing page) was famous, and Antique copies of this panel, which flanked a small entrance stairway at the west, still survive. The reliefs repeated the same theme several times: Nikes bring sacrificial bulls and erect trophies in the presence of Athena.

   The single theme of "Victory," which dominated the temple and balustrade, was in painful contradiction to the actual course of events. The Peloponnesian War (431–404 B.C.) consumed the strength of Athens and ended with her complete collapse. For this reason, the eye took even greater pleasure not only in the theme but in the beauty of an art which combined soft forms and flowing lines into an image of a joyful, enchanting world.

Temple of Athena Nike. Marble. c. 420 B.C. To the right of the entrance to the Athenian Acropolis (see page 128)

Nike Unlacing Her Sandal. Marble, height 41³/₄″. c. 420 B.C. From the balustrade of the temple of Athena Nike, Athens. Acropolis Museum, Athens

The style used here by this North Greek artist is very close to that of the Nike balustrade and other Attic works. Technically, too, this marble statue of a Nike, originally over nine and a half feet high, is a masterpiece. The inscription on the socket reads: "The Messenians and the Naupaktians dedicated her to the Olympian Zeus as a tithe of the enemy's booty. Paionios of Mende made her and was also victorious in the construction of the temple acroteria." Pausanias (V, 26, 1) confirmed this inscription and reported that, contrary to his own opinion, the Messenians themselves relate the dedication to a victory at Sphakteria in the year 421. A flying eagle at the feet of the goddess and the painting of the figure (which has now disappeared) reinforced the impression of hovering flight. The wind blows out the cloak behind her, which was also carved from the same block of marble.

Six maenads, some holding dismembered animals, are shown on the wall of the krater on the facing page, one of the rare examples of metalwork of this period. Athens is the most likely place of origin.

Flying Nike, by Paionios. Marble, height 85″. Formerly on a column c. 295′ high facing the east side of the temple of Zeus at Olympia. c. 420 B.C. Museum, Olympia

Maenads in Ecstasy, detail of a krater. Bronze, over-all height formerly c. 17³/₄″, height of frieze 7⁷/₈″, with the ornament, 11″. Silver and copper inlay on the ornamentation and on the maenads (hair bands, arm rings). c. 410 B.C. From South Russia (probably from a mound near Maikop). State Museums, Berlin

This over life-size statue had been broken up and used as filling in a late Roman fortification wall. It epitomizes, in the treatment of the drapery, the animated style of the late fifth century B.C. with its "baroque" exaggeration, and is a typical tour de force of the same style that gave added beauty to figures on vases and reliefs, and thus also to the works of art themselves. It suggests the sculptor Kallimachos, who is also said to have "invented" the Corinthian capital (Vitruvius, IV, I, 9–10). However, the virtuoso mastery of the technique of carving in marble required by the Corinthian capital was not limited to any one sculptor but was necessary for the realization of almost all artistic ideas. Of course painting, which reached its apogee with Timanthes, Zeuxis, and Parrhasios, was free of such technical problems.

The superficial stylistic features of large-scale painting of the late fifth century B.C. were reflected in Attic vase painting. The principal scene of the hydria on the facing page shows Athena and Hera standing at the left, Paris and Hermes in the center, and on the right (in the detail shown) Aphrodite seated with her attendants and her son Eros, while the sun-god's horses rise up above them. In the band below are represented satyrs and maenads with Dionysos. The style is close to that of Meidias, one of the leading vase painters of the time.

Aphrodite at the Judgment of Paris. Detail of an Attic hydria. Terra cotta with glaze paint and gilding, over-all height of the vase $19^1/_2$″. Late fifth century B.C. From Ruvo (southern Italy). Badisches Landesmuseum, Karlsruhe

Aphrodite. Marble, height 72″. c. 410 B.C. From the Agora, Athens. Agora Museum, Athens

Hegeso and a Servant. Attic grave stele. Marble, height 58⁵/₈". c. 400 B.C. From the Dipylon cemetery, Athens. National Museum, Athens

The series of Attic tomb reliefs, which had already struck a tenderly human note in Archaic times (see page 107), re-emerged at the end of the fifth century B.C. with masterpieces such as the stele of Hegeso. The inscription beneath the pediment bears only the names of the dead Hegeso and of her father (or husband) Proxenos. She chooses a piece of jewelry (once painted) from a casket held by her maid. Yet, the real subject of the relief, which combines a modern beauty of line with the calm of Pheidian art, is the loveliness of life and sorrow over its end.

Youth Sacrificing ("Idolino"). Copy (or cast) of a bronze original from the circle of Polykleitos. Bronze, height 58¹/₄". Original c. 410 B.C. From Pesaro (Italy). Museo Nazionale Archeologico, Florence

The "discoveries" of Polykleitos and his circle continued to influence and, on the whole, determine the appearance of statues of youths. From different angles, the *"Idolino"* reveals either the rather awkward stance of the boy or the linear beauty and elegance of his body. Similar figures on contemporary grave reliefs are also striking for the pleasing quality of their relaxed aspect and their peculiar elegiac mood. This is strengthened here by the impression that the boy's thoughts are on other matters. This conflict, psychologically observed by Euripides, determines the new "ethos" of works of art of the period, which saw the "classic" world of Periklean Athens crumble.

Medea and the Daughters of Pelias. Copy of a marble relief, probably from the "Altar of Compassion" on the Athenian Agora. Marble, height 42$^1/_2$". Original c. 410 B.C. Museo Profano Lateranense, Rome

This relief depicting the daughters of Pelias following Medea's counsel and preparing to cut their father to pieces in order to rejuvenate him is one of a series of four which take psychological conflict, the turning point between hope and doubt, as their theme. They can probably be related to the Sicilian expedition (413 B.C.) which sealed the decline of Athenian might. The funeral dirge for those who fell before Syracuse was composed by Euripides, and these reliefs seem inspired by the same Euripidean spirit.

THE FOURTH CENTURY (400–320 B.C.)

Like the wars between Athens, Sparta, and Thebes, the political catastrophe that resulted in the end of Athenian supremacy brought about a turning away from political life and toward that of the individual. The relationships between compatible minds, between members of a family, between friends, and the awareness which Sokrates had awakened of the self-responsibility of the individual now took first place. In art, this led to a new concept of the figures of heroes and gods. They are seen and interpreted as men but are raised up to an ideal sphere, where they exist as higher beings. The intellectual powers of the Greeks in the fourth century B.C. turned toward art and philosophy, and their achievements in these fields have survived over the centuries. The separation of the individual from the state was the prerequisite for this new concentration on art and philosophy: now that this had taken place, the state was dispensable to the individual.

Dexileos. Grave stele. Marble, height with base 68$^7/_8$". The bridle, reins, spear, and wreath in Dexileos' hair, and the sword belt of the fallen warrior were of bronze. Shortly after 394 B.C. From the Dipylon cemetery, Athens. Kerameikos Museum, Athens

The inscription on the slightly concave base of the stele above informs us that Dexileos of Thorikos distinguished himself in battle at Corinth and was killed there at the age of twenty. He is shown victoriously galloping over a fallen enemy, yet his eyes already hold a presentiment of imminent death. The models for both figures can be found in Pheidean art, and it is probable that the artist was deliberately inviting comparison with it. The Battle of Corinth in 394 B.C., in which Dexileos fell, is a little-known conflict between Athens and Sparta. In its great effort to recover from the political collapse brought about by the Peloponnesian War, Athens fought Sparta and aimed, like Thebes, at political supremacy in Greece. The victory of King Philip II of Macedon at Chaironeia in 338 B.C. brought these wars to an end and heralded the age of Alexander the Great.

The regularity of the encircling columns, the lack of corners and angles, as well as the more intimate character of a round temple set up high on a circular base explain the popularity which this type of building enjoyed in the fourth century B.C.

The rotunda in Delphi had twenty Doric columns, each of whose twenty flutes repeated the outlines of the ground plan. Inside, ten Corinthian columns raised up on a continuous socle were set directly against the wall of the cella. The metopes were decorated with battles of Amazons and centaurs, the sima (gutter molding) with acanthus scrolls, palmettes, and lion-head spouts. The architect, Theodoros of Phokaia, wrote a book about this little temple, his masterpiece (Vitruvius, VII, 12).

Tholos of the Sanctuary of Athena Pronaia, Delphi, by Theodoros of Phokaia. Marble, cella floor and socle for the columns of dark Eleusinian limestone. Diameter of the cella 28′ 2⁵/₈″, height to the sima 27′ 2¹/₂″. c. 390 B.C.

Nike (?). Bronze, formerly gilded, height 9¹/₂″. Early fourth century B.C. From the Athenian Agora. Agora Museum, Athens

This bronze original, somewhat over half life-size, has lost the chignon on top of its head, the eyes, and the gilded silver foil which covered the bronze surfaces and was fastened at each side of the neck in a vertical groove.

The convincing, tender treatment of the hair and the small face dominated by the large eyes are indications of a new ideal and of a new striving by the artist to penetrate the surface in order to reveal the inner being.

Leda and the Swan. Copy of bronze original, probably by Timotheos. Marble, height 52″. Original c. 370 B.C. Capitoline Museum, Rome

This masterpiece, which has survived in countless copies, is attributed to Timotheos, although ancient literature makes no reference to a *Leda* by this sculptor. Stylistically it matches the sculptures from Epidauros (see facing page) where Timotheos is known to have worked. The artist has added an emotional dimension to the physical theme of Leda's amorous encounter with Zeus transformed into a swan. The figure of Leda expresses compassion for the swan (seemingly threatened by an eagle), childish innocence, and fear coupled with a sudden recognition of the god.

Aura. Acroterium from the temple of Asklepios, Epidauros. Marble, height 31¼". c. 380 B.C. National Museum, Athens

Maidens on horseback, identified as wind-goddesses, decorated the corners of the temple pediments. The building inscription states that the acroteria on one side were executed by Timotheos, those on the other side by an otherwise unknown sculptor named Theodotos. Since Timotheos, the most important sculptor, would be more likely to have done the principal east side, this mounted Aura is no longer attributed to him but to Theodotos. Even though it is unlikely, therefore, that Timotheos himself made this figure, he would have determined the style, for (as is stated in the inscription) he provided the "*typoi,*" that is, the working models for the sculptural decoration.

Athena. Copy of bronze original by Timotheos (?). Marble, height 64⅛″. Original c. 375 B.C. State Museums, Berlin

The goddess shown here has the same human quality as in the votive relief from the Acropolis (see page 141). The imposing grandeur of the Pheidian *Athenas* (see pages 153, 158) has given way once more to a more girlish appearance. The sculptor was probably Timotheos, judging from the similarity between the head of this *Athena* and that of *Leda* (see page 182). The traditional name of the statue, *Athena as a Young Girl,* is quite appropriate. However, since ancient sources make no mention of this work, the surprising turn of the goddess' head has not yet been explained. There is a hint of shyness in her stance which seems to be emphasized by her upward glance.

The satyr pouring wine into a cup is probably a reproduction of Praxiteles' *Satyr,* which stood in the Street of the Tripods in Athens (see page 207) and which Praxiteles considered his best work. In some replicas the statue was so constructed that water could be made to flow through pipes from the jug into the cup.

Art connoisseurs of Antiquity rated Praxiteles as one of the greatest sculptors, alongside Pheidias, Polykleitos, Myron, and Lysippos; and his fame far surpassed that of any of his contemporaries. The art of the fourth century B.C. reached its apogee in the sculptures of Praxiteles, of which the *Aphrodite of Knidos* was the most admired (see page 188). It is more difficult for us today to appreciate his art than it was in 1877, when the discovery of his Hermes (see page 187) was accompanied by extravagant praise. This affinity with the taste of the late nineteenth century caused his works to be judged in a false, sickly-sweet light, which makes it hard for us to discard these concepts and gain a fresh appreciation of the art of Praxiteles. Even if he considers them the creations of a "second classic" period, the modern observer, schooled in Archaic and classical sculpture, cannot help doing them an injustice, even if unintentionally. There remains a value judgment that feels obliged to discern negative qualities in these works. This may, perhaps, be excused by circumstances, but it is certainly just as wrong as the thoughtless projection of nineteenth-century personal ideals into the sculptures of Praxiteles. The statues might be called sentimental, were it not for the ambiguous meaning of the term. The same holds true for the assertion that Praxiteles took into consideration, in a hitherto unknown way, the effect of his work on the observer. Yet, the artist does envelop his marble statues in a veil of quiet reflection which, by withdrawing the figures from the world of reality, draws the viewer into the statues' own world. It is not surprising that the art of Praxiteles exerted such a strong influence on tomb reliefs (see page 202). The painter Nikias (see pages 204–6), whom Praxiteles so highly esteemed, exerted a similar influence.

Satyr Pouring Wine. Copy of an original by Praxiteles. Marble, height $57^{1}/_{8}''$. Original c. 370 B.C. Staatliche Kunstsammlungen, Dresden

Apollo Sauroktonos. Copy of the original by Praxiteles. Marble, height 65³/₄″ (from the top of the head to the soles of the feet, 60¹/₄″). Original c. 350 B.C. From the Palatine, Rome. Vatican Museums, Rome

The "Apollo as a boy, teasing a lizard with an arrow, the so-called *Sauroktonos*" (Pliny 34, 70), listed among the works of Praxiteles, was frequently copied, despite the technical difficulties presented by the subject. The tree is both an integral part of the composition and a technically necessary support for the slender figure of Apollo. Why it was that Praxiteles represented the god in this boyish form, apparently playing a cruel child's game with the lizard, remains a mystery. The wishes of the patron and the demands of the cult would have been the determining factors.

Hermes with the Child Dionysos, by Praxiteles. Marble, height 84⁵/₈″. c. 330 B.C. From the Heraion of Olympia. Museum, Olympia

The statue was found in 1877 just where Pausanias had seen it (V, 17, 3). The "marble Hermes, carrying the child Dionysos, a work by Praxiteles" is one of the few surviving originals of the master. The virtuosity apparent in the treatment of the marble and the over-all elegance of the work confirm ancient opinions on the art of Praxiteles. Hermes has stopped to rest on his way to the nymphs who will take care of his infant brother Dionysos. He leans on a tree trunk to play with the child and offers him a cluster of grapes. The fatherly concern displayed by this childish game shows Hermes, the messenger of the gods, in a moment of almost feminine affection, and reveals a new facet of the god to the observer.

Aphrodite of Knidos. Copy of the original by Praxiteles. Marble, overall height of the statue 80¹/₄″. Original c. 350 B.C. Vatican Museums, Rome

Praxiteles is said to have surpassed himself in his *Aphrodite of Knidos.* Pliny writes (36, 30) that many people suffered the hardships of an ocean voyage just for a view of her; and other writers also praised the statue, which showed the goddess completely naked for the first time. Her rapt gaze was particularly admired. The goddess, who is preparing for her bath, seems herself to have fallen under the spell of the forces that she embodies. However, this human quality is countered by her consciousness of the magic powers that she exerts on the beholder, and elevates her to a new ideal of divinity.

188

Artemis. Copy, probably of the *Artemis Brauronia* by Praxiteles. Marble, height 65". Original c. 340 B.C. From Gabii, near Rome. The Louvre, Paris

The goddess is shown in the act of fastening her mantle. This unusual motif supports the identification of this statue with the work of Praxiteles, since temple inventories indicate that offerings of garments were made to the *Artemis Brauronia* on the Athenian Acropolis, where the statue by Praxiteles stood (Pausanias I, 23, 7). The importance placed upon an insignificant act, which also reveals the huntress Artemis as a girl who delights in new clothing, wholly corresponds to the Praxitelean interpretation of the traditional concept of the gods. As in all Praxiteles' works, the garments show no trace of the ornately flowing line of the turn of the century (see page 174), which was long retained in decorative works. With the techniques of classical art, Praxiteles has tried to capture the texture of the cloth garments, whose natural weight causes the folds to hang vertically down.

189

The style of the *Aphrodite* on the facing page, the lower part of whose body is draped, identifies it as the work of Praxiteles, who is known to have made several other statues of the same goddess in addition to the Knidian one. This *Aphrodite* may be somewhat earlier in date, although the differences between the two interpretations may rather lie in the fact that the artist has simply chosen to show here another aspect of the many-faceted nature of the goddess of love.

On the outside of the mirror case below, a relief of a clothed Aphrodite shows her seated next to an Eros, who is drawing his bow. The incised design on the inside of the cover, however, shows the goddess of love in all her naked beauty, lovingly holding the little Eros close to her—and interfering with his aim.

Aphrodite. Copy of an original by Praxiteles. Marble, over-all height of the statue 76³/₈″. Original c. 350 B.C. From Arles. The Louvre, Paris

Aphrodite and Eros. Inner decoration of a folding mirror. Gilt bronze, diameter 7¹/₂″. c. 350 B.C. From Tarquinia. The Louvre, Paris

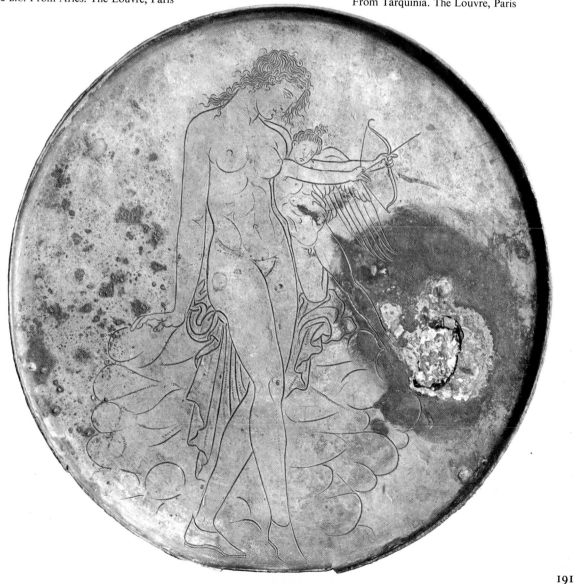

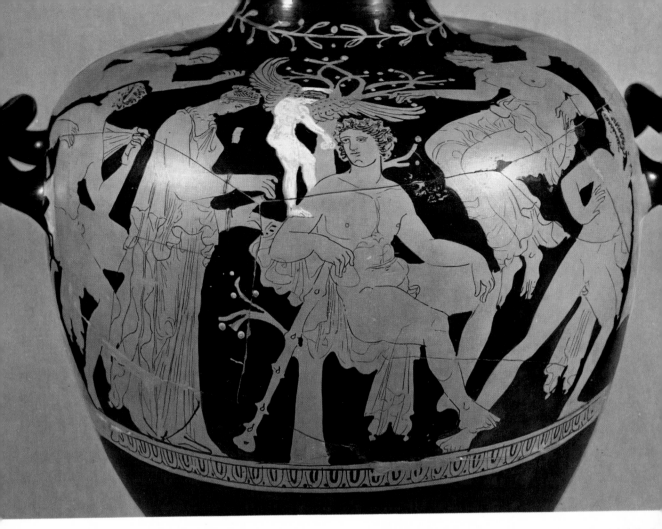

Herakles in the Garden of the Hesperides. Attic hydria. Terra cotta with glaze paint, white color, and gilding, height 15½". c. 350 B.C. From Cyrene, North Africa. British Museum, London

A Hero. Bronze, the eyes inlaid in colored material, height ▶ 76⅜". c. 350 B.C. From the sea near Antikythera (island off the southern Peloponnesus). National Museum, Athens

The bringing together of apparently unconnected figures is typical of the Attic vases which were exported to southern Russia ("Kerch vases") and North Africa. The tree in the middle and the small Eros identify the four maidens, for whom Herakles seems to be searching, as the Hesperides; but this does not explain the other figures.

 This class of vases marked the end of Attic vase painting, and pottery reverted once more to ornamental decoration. The technically more demanding vessels of bronze (see page 208) or of precious metal now came to the forefront.

The young man (facing page) extends his right arm, the half-closed hand of which seems to have held some small object. All attempts to identify either the subject matter or the hero, who has paused in mid-stride, have so far met with little success. The statue sank to the bottom of the sea when it was shipwrecked on its way to Italy in the first century B.C.

The figure of the hero, which completely dominates the picture, has the appearance of a statue. Theseus is enthusiastically greeted by liberated Athenian children after he has killed the Minotaur. Still affected by his battle with the monster, which lies dead at his feet, he gazes out into the distance and seems, despite the presence of the crowd, isolated and tragic. In the Praxitelean sense, the scene merely serves as an occasion for making the hero more movingly human.

Theseus after Killing the Minotaur.
Roman copy of an original of c.
350 B.C. Height 31$^7/_8$". Wall painting
from the House of Gavius Rufus,
Pompeii. Museo Nazionale, Naples

Head of a Hero. From a pediment
of the temple of Athena Alea in
Tegea. Marble, height 8$^1/_4$". After
395 B.C. National Museum, Athens

Next to Praxiteles, Skopas of Paros was the outstanding sculptor of the fourth century B.C. He was also active
as an architect and, in 395 B.C., rebuilt the temple of Athena Alea in Tegea, which had been destroyed by fire.
The pediment sculptures, countless fragments of which have survived, can be considered his. Pausanias (VIII,
45, 4) describes the themes of the pediments: on the east side, the hunt of the Calydonian boar with Atalante,
Meleager, Theseus, and other heroes; on the west, Telephos and Achilles fighting in the Plain of Kaikos.

The forceful emotions shown in the heads reveal Skopas as an outstanding master of the power of expression.
He raised human passions to a sublime pathos and demonstrated in his work the tragic imperfection of man—
and even of the hero. In his efforts to depict the spiritual, he seems to have joined paths with Praxiteles, whose
figures are, however, more introverted in contrast to the more openly extrovert figures of Skopas. These seem
to strike a responsive chord in the emotions of the viewer and demand his sympathy. Funerary reliefs were
strongly influenced by the art of Skopas (see page 202).

Pothos. Roman copy of an original by Skopas. Marble, height (without base) 5′ 11″. Original c. 350 B.C. From the Via Cavour, Rome. Palazzo dei Conservatori, Rome

Skopas made two statues of Eros' brother Pothos, the personification of desire—one for Samothrace (Pliny 36, 25) and one for Megara (Pausanias I, 43, 6). This frequently copied statue of a standing youth leaning on one upraised arm, his legs crossed, his languishing eyes set in soft, almost effeminate features, can therefore be attributed to Skopas. The personification of a human passion is quite in line with Skopasian art (see page 195), which was particularly attracted by the conflict between man's desires and his capabilities, and by his consequent longing to overcome his own limitations. Here, the whole body, as well as the expression, of Pothos seems to be set on a far-off, longed-for goal.

Maenad. Roman copy of an original by Skopas. Marble, height 17³/₄″. Original c. 350 B.C. Staatliche Kunstsammlungen, Dresden

The *Maenad* of Skopas, so highly praised by the ancient poets, was carved out of Parian marble. It showed at one and the same time the feminine beauty of the girl with her long flowing hair and the rapture of the orgiastic maenad as she tears an animal in pieces (see page 173). It was the epitome of demoniac ecstasy.

This Roman copy probably reproduces Skopas' masterpiece, for this maenad, as no other, is the very personification of Dionysiac frenzy.

197

The Rape of Ganymede. Relief on a folding mirror, perhaps originally fastened to a vessel. Bronze, diameter c. 6″. c. 360 B.C. From the vicinity of Amphissa. State Museums, Berlin

The art of the fourth century B.C., so decidedly feminine in its leanings, was particularly enamored of objects related to the feminine toilette. The folding mirrors are decorated on the outside of the cover with reliefs and often on the inside with incised designs (see page 191). The themes revolve primarily around love. In the example shown here, the youth willingly follows the eagle of Zeus to Olympus, and one senses in the relief something of the longing of man for the higher, ideal world of Plato's philosophy.

Mausolos (?). Marble, height 9′ 10¹/₈″. Carian, 350 B.C. From the Mausoleum of Halikarnassos. British Museum, London

This is undoubtedly the statue of a Carian prince, either a relative of Mausolos or Mausolos himself. The corpulence and the long hair give the figure a "barbaric" appearance. It was part of the wealth of sculptural decoration on the tomb monument erected by Artemisia for her deceased husband Mausolos, from which the word "mausoleum" is derived. The princes of Asia Minor competed with each other in the splendor of their burial places and employed Greek artists for this purpose. Since this statue was found at the northern side of the structure, it would, according to Pliny's classification (see page 200), be the work of Bryaxis.

Amazonomachy. Fragment of the relief decoration of the
Mausoleum of Halikarnassos. Marble, height 35″. c. 350
B.C. British Museum, London

The architects of the Mausoleum of Halikarnassos, one of the Seven Wonders of the World, were Pytheos and Satyros; and the most famous sculptors of the time executed the rich sculptural decoration. Pliny (36, 30) states that Timotheos was responsible for the southern side, Skopas the east front, Bryaxis the north side, and Leochares the west; but this division is probably oversimplified. It is impossible to attribute any of the surviving reliefs with certainty to a particular hand, since their original position in the structure cannot always be definitely determined, and since there are no obvious stylistic differences between the various reliefs. Added to this is the fact that, since Vitruvius names Praxiteles instead of Timotheos, there is not even agreement as to the names of the artists. Leochares was probably the youngest, since he and Lysippos were the leading artists of the time of Alexander the Great (see page 219).

All we can say about this scene, which also includes the figures of Herakles, Hades, and Persephone, is that it takes place in the underworld. The temple of Artemis at Ephesos, another of the Wonders of the World, was over three hundred and fifty feet long and was surrounded by a double row of columns. Some of these had relief decoration on their lower parts, and one is said to have been the work of Skopas. This relief has affinities with the style of various masters of the fourth century B.C.

Thanatos, Alkestis, and Hermes. Column drum carved in relief from the new temple of Artemis in Ephesos rebuilt after the fire of 356 B.C. Marble, height 70⁷/₈″. British Museum, London

Demetria and Pamphile. Tomb relief. Marble on a prosoporos base, height 84⁵/₈". Mid-fourth century B.C. Dipylon cemetery, Athens

The standing Demetria and the seated Pamphile in the foreground turn out of the relief toward the observer, in sharp contrast to the withdrawn quality of the Hegeso stele (see page 176). The two women (sisters or friends?) seem isolated in much the same way as the figures in the paintings of Nikias (see pages 204–6), each individually seeking to detain the passer-by with her glance. The inscription on the grave statue of Kroisos (see page 110) admonished the viewer to "stand and mourn," but now it is the figures themselves that invite compassion. This class of funerary relief seems to reveal the influence of Skopasian art (see page 195).

Demeter sits on a throne, clothed in rich garments whose folds lie diagonally across her body. The blocklike ▶ appearance of the whole is softened by the slant of the left lower leg, by the drapery on the upper part of the body, and by the turn of the head. It has not yet been possible to attribute this original work to any particular sculptor, although it has certain affinities with Praxiteles and with his *Aphrodite* from the same island (see page 188), for instance, the goddess' gaze into the infinite distance. Despite the fact that she would be oblivious to her daughter Kore (who was probably standing beside her), she is, in contrast to the *Aphrodite,* the epitome of motherliness, that other side of feminine nature.

Demeter Enthroned. Marble,
height 60¼". c. 340 B.C. From
Knidos. British Museum, London

The fourth century B.C. is the classic century of painting: both the great admiration later accorded paintings from this period and the fact that copies of them were made are evidence of this.

Pliny (35, 131) lists an *Andromeda* among the paintings by Nikias, and it is probable that the Pompeian painter of the picture above used it as a model. The lack of action in the scene is unusual. Andromeda has not yet been freed from her bonds, and neither she nor her rescuer shows any sign of joy—in fact, they do not even look at each other. The similarity of mood between such a painting and the statues of Praxiteles (see page 185) makes the close association of these two artists, mentioned by the writers of Antiquity, plausible. Nikias is said to have done the painting on some of Praxiteles' marble statues, and these are the very ones that Praxiteles is said to have regarded as his most successful.

Io, whom Zeus loved and who was turned into a cow by Hera, is watched over by the giant Argos in this companion piece to the painting of Kalypso in the same room (see page 206). An *Io* is mentioned by Pliny (35, 131) as being among the works of Nikias. In all the paintings of Nikias that are identified only by the name of the woman portrayed, the real theme is the contrasting thoughts with which she and her male companion are occupied.

These paintings are not pictorial narratives but psychological character studies. The imminent arrival of Hermes to free Io is not indicated in any way and, unlike the well-known version of the myth, the relationship here of the guardian to his prisoner is human and not without compassion.

Odysseus and Kalypso. Roman copy of an original by Nikias (?). Height $32^1/_4$". Original c. 340 B.C. Wall painting in the Macellum, Pompeii

Pliny (35, 131) mentions a *Kalypso* by Nikias, and the interpretation of the standing woman in this picture as Kalypso is most probable. The homesick Odysseus and the nymph who is unwilling to see him go provide the picture with that inner tension apparently characteristic of Nikias.

By restricting the number of principal figures to two, Nikias avoided superfluous details and the essence of the picture is immediately made clear. The mythical figures force the observer to think their thoughts, to place himself in their situation. The setting is almost always the same: two people, a man and a woman, meet more or less by chance—certainly not on purpose—and their ways will soon separate. Pervading all, and keeping the two apart even in their moment of meeting, are the tragic bonds which tie their existence to a predetermined path. The combination of two figures belonging to different spheres is echoed in grave reliefs, where the living and the dead appear side by side.

Choragic monument of Lysikrates. Marble on limestone podium, height 34'. 334 B.C. Street of the Tripods, Athens

According to the inscription, this monument was dedicated by Lysikrates, whose boys' choir won the musical competition under the archon Euainetos (see page 143). It is in the form of a small circular temple with six Corinthian columns rising on a square podium. Tripods are sculptured in relief on the upper portion of the walls between the columns, and a large gilded tripod once crowned the whole above the acanthus ornament on the top. On the frieze are representations of Dionysos, of the satyrs' pursuit of the pirates, and of their transformation into dolphins.

The round temple (see page 180) has here become a high, almost columnar, pedestal for the tripod, which was the actual votive offering. This demonstrates that it was the beauty and individuality of the architecture that counted, even when its true function had become obscured.

Painted pottery could no longer satisfy the demands of the time for ever more sumptuous vases (see page 192). Archaic art had produced bronze vessels with appliqué figures, and in the fifth century B.C. metal cups, kraters, and bowls, all with relief decoration, were made by outstanding artists (see page 173). Wealthy Macedonia now promoted this art of ornamented metalwork, which supplanted pottery.

This krater with its rich decoration of reliefs and applied figures was found in a grave. Asteiounios of Larissa, son of Anaxagoras, who is named in the inscription, was probably the owner of this magnificent mixing bowl, and he may also have been the artist. The decoration shows Dionysos and Ariadne and the reveling companions of the wine-god.

Despite its rich ornamentation, the bowl does not appear overladen. The relief has been kept within the general outline of the vase and the figures in the round are organically related to the shoulders of the krater. The whole forms a unity which reveals the great skill of the craftsman.

Achilles and Briseis. Roman copy ▶ of an original painting of c. 330 B.C. Height 50″. Wall painting from the House of the Tragic Poet, Pompeii. Museo Nazionale, Naples

Krater. Bronze, partly silvered, height 35⁷/₈″. c. 340 B.C. From Dherveni (Macedonia). Archaeological Museum, Saloniki

The unknown painter has created, in this picture of the enforced separation of Briseis from Achilles, a somber mood illuminated only by the heroic bearing of the impassive Achilles and the pitiful figure of the beautiful slave girl. The impending disaster has already been foreseen by the participants in the scene, and Briseis' impelling glance draws in the observer as well. The emphasis placed on Achilles and the other main characters by means of the background figures, the momentariness of the situation, and the gestures are sure signs that the original came into being under the auspices of the new order instigated by Alexander the Great.

THE LATE GREEK ART OF ALEXANDER'S EMPIRE (336–146 B.C.)

Late Greek art is a mirror image of the historical state of affairs that was determined by the greatest expansion of Greek political might. The focal point lies in the period of the reign of Alexander the Great (336–323 B.C.) and of his immediate successors (the Diadochi, 323–280 B.C., and the Epigones, c. 280–220 B.C.). The end is marked by the Roman conquest of Greece and Macedonia in the year 146 B.C. This period of almost two centuries of artistic production was considered the apogee of Greek art by the ancients. In the century that followed, art was still nourished by this rich tradition, so that fine works of art were produced and the courts of the East Greek princes were provided with their necessary splendor. But in reality, this was only a passive phase leading to the end of Greek art, which now continued on Italian soil. This transferral of the Greek art of the East to the West, where it could win a new life, led to the somewhat primitive view of Pliny (34, 52) that art had stopped after the disciples of Lysippos and had not reawakened until about 155 B.C.

The term "Hellenistic," which is still used today for this late period of Greek art, is misleading. "Hellenism" as a concept comes from historiography and comprises the time between the death of Alexander and the beginning of the reign of Augustus. The attempt to classify the art of these three centuries as a unit and then to split it up into subdivisions was doomed to failure, for this method disregarded historic conditions and was based only on formal criteria which could not do justice to the great variety of Late Greek art. Even from a linguistic standpoint the term "Hellenistic" is improper. It was originated by the historian J. G. Droysen, who introduced it into historiography in 1836. "Hellenistai" (*Acts*, VI, 1), as opposed to the "Hebrews," were Hellenized Jews who spoke Greek. The word is also commonly used by those who make Hellenism a synonym for Grecism. Late Greek art, however, is Greek art—not Hellenized—and therefore not Hellenistic. The term has also been applied to the feeble end and collapse that took place after Greek art had long ceased to place itself in the services of those princes who continued to live a shadow existence in complete dependence on the real rulers of the world.

Battle of Alexander and Darius. Copy of an original painting by Apelles (?). Mosaic, 8′ 10³/₄″ × 16′ 9⁵/₈″. Original c. 325 B.C. Floor mosaic from the House of the Faun, Pompeii. Museo Nazionale, Naples

This gigantic mosaic is our only faithful copy of an Antique battle painting. The exact historical event (usually identified as the Battle of Issos) cannot, however, be determined with certainty; for the picture is meant as an idealization of a battle, in which the elan of the attacking King of Macedonia is contrasted with the cowardice of the fleeing Persian king. No doubt the original painting belonged to a cycle that narrated the life of Alexander from his birth to his final victory. Later ages continued to produce works based on these originals, such as Alexander's schooling, the burning of Persepolis, the fight with the lion, and his marriage to Roxana (see page 213).

The incongruities of the mosaic can be explained as misinterpretations on the part of the artist of various parts of the original painting, which had apparently already been damaged.

Alexander in Battle. Frieze on the so-called *Alexander Sarcophagus*. Marble with rich painting, height of the frieze 27⁵/₈″, over-all length of the sarcophagus, 10′ 5¹/₄″. c. 310 B.C. From Sidon. Archaeological Museum, Istanbul

Found in a burial chamber in the royal necropolis of Sidon, this sarcophagus probably belonged to King Abdalonymos, whom Alexander had set on the throne. One side shows Alexander at the battle of Issos; the other, a lion hunt. Scenes of combat and of the chase also decorate the ends and the pediments. The style reveals an artist who deliberately and harmoniously "classicized" motifs such as that of the *Battle of Alexander* painting (see page 211). The rich ornamentation was also executed with exceptional delicacy.

The new ideal of the warrior battling against enemies and wild beasts is in complete conformity with widespread old Greek ideas that were expressed as far back as Mycenaean times (see pages 34, 42).

Images such as these on coins and gems probably represent details of paintings glorifying Alexander and his deeds (see page 211). The *Alexander with the Thunderbolt* was a famous painting by Apelles that was frequently mentioned by the writers of Antiquity. (The inscription on the gem below refers to a later owner.)

The obverse of the gold coin shows Alexander on horseback attacking the Indian king Poros, who attempts to parry the thrust of Alexander's lance from his elephant. On the reverse, Alexander, holding the thunderbolt of Zeus, is crowned by Nike.

Obverse and reverse of a coin (decadrachm) of Alexander the Great. Gold, diameter 1¹/₄". c. 320 B.C. British Museum, London

◀ Gem representing Alexander with the attributes of Zeus. Carnelian, height 1¹/₈". c. 325 B.C. The Hermitage, Leningrad

Herakles Resting (so-called *Farnese Herakles*). Copy, by Glykon of Athens, of the bronze original of Lysippos. Marble, height 10′ 4³/₄″. Original c. 330 B.C. Museo Nazionale, Naples

For Antiquity, Greek sculpture reached its climax in the figures of Lysippos. Basing his work on earlier attempts and on the Polykleitan system (see page 162), which he improved, he freed Greek sculpture from the last of its bonds. Together with Leochares (see pages 200, 219), who also received commissions from Alexander, Lysippos headed a large school of students, imitators, and followers, and prepared the way for the art of the third century B.C.

Although this colossal statue (facing page) bears the signature of the copyist, an inscription on a replica in Florence describes it as "the work of Lysippos." The artist has shown Herakles as he rests on his club, exhausted by his labors. One might be justified in interpreting it as an allusion to the superhuman efforts which the ideals of the times expected of a hero.

This statuette of the seated Herakles with a drinking cup in his right hand (rather than the apples added by the restorer) reproduces the silver *Herakles* which Lysippos presented to Alexander the Great. There is no reason to doubt that the original was a table ornament, even though the piece later known to have been owned by Novius Vindex may have been only a copy. According to the poets Martial and Statius, Lysippos' Herakles looked up at the stars and invited the guests to the joys of the festive meal.

Herakles Epitrapezios. Copy of the silver original by Lysippos. Marble, height 20⁷/₈". Original c. 330 B.C. British Museum, London

Athletes. Detail of a sculptured statue base from the Athenian Acropolis. Marble, over-all height 18⁷/₈″, length 63³/₄″, width 35⁷/₈″. c. 320 B.C. Acropolis Museum, Athens

Apoxyomenos. Copy of the bronze original by Lysippos. Marble, height 80³/₄″. Original c. 330 B.C. From the Tiber in Rome. Vatican Museums, Rome

The works of Lysippos and the new interest that he aroused in the human body and in athletics strongly influenced almost all monuments of Late Greek art.

A frieze of athletes, whose names are inscribed beside them, runs along three sides of the plinth above. They have been caught in various poses as they cleanse themselves with the strigil (scraper), and give the effect of being real-life studies. The statue which once stood on this base may have resembled the *Apoxyomenos* (see facing page).

In the greater vivacity and slender proportions of the figure, the *Apoxyomenos* is the best example of Lysippos' new style. The athlete cleansing himself with a scraper dominates the surrounding space as never before. It is evident that Lysippos returned to works of the early fifth century B.C. (see page 129) for his inspiration, rejecting the art of the immediate past. The fact that only one marble copy of this work exists is probably due to the technical difficulties involved. This copy had a strut between the right thigh and the outstretched right arm, which was most disturbing and which also required a disproportionately large block of marble. The *Apoxyomenos* of Lysippos was mentioned by Pliny (34, 62).

Apollo (so-called *Apollo Belvedere*).
Copy of a bronze original by Leochares
(?). Marble, height 98$^{1}/_{8}$″. Original c.
330 B.C. From Anzio-Nettuno (?). Belvedere, Vatican Museums, Rome

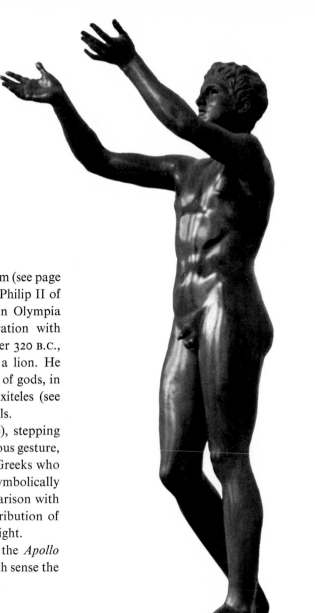

Leochares is said to have worked on the Mausoleum (see page 200) and to have made gold and ivory statues of Philip II of Macedon and his family for a round temple in Olympia (the Philippeion). He also created, in collaboration with Lysippos, a bronze group dedicated in Delphi after 320 B.C., which showed Krateros saving Alexander from a lion. He seems to have been a master in the representation of gods, in which, like Pheidias (see pages 153–55) and Praxiteles (see pages 185–90) before him, he established new ideals.

This new type of the god Apollo (facing page), stepping lightly forward and holding up his bow in a victorious gesture, seems to correspond to the self-awareness of the Greeks who conquered the world with Alexander. Apollo symbolically expresses the spirit of Greek culture, which comparison with Oriental concepts had set in a new light. The attribution of this masterpiece to Leochares is almost certainly right.

The reactions of Winckelmann and Goethe to the *Apollo Belvedere* were equally enthusiastic: they could both sense the greatness of the original in this rather poor copy.

Like the art of Lysippos, that of Leochares also had widespread effects, as can be seen in this figure of a youth in Berlin. The boy lifted both arms (which were missing and have been restored) high above his head, and may have held a victor's fillet. The apparent weightlessness of the figure, in particular, is typically Leocharian. His statue of *Ganymede* is an outstanding example of this quality, but it is also present in the figure of *Apollo* (facing page).

Standing Youth. Copy of a bronze original of c. 320 B.C. Bronze, height 50$\frac{3}{8}$". State Museums, Berlin

Aristonautes. Marble, height 84¼" (with the base, 9' 4¼"). c. 330 B.C. From the Dipylon cemetery, Athens. National Museum, Athens

◀ The influence of painting on funerary art is evident in the tombstone of Aristonautes. The motif of a warrior rushing out of the background also appeared in a painting by Theon. This is described by Aelian (*Var. Hist.,* II, 44), who comments that every time the painter unveiled the picture he had trumpets blown so as to heighten the effect on the public. The impression produced by this monument—one of the latest of Attic funerary reliefs (see page 225), and the only example of its kind—is that of a sculpture in the round set into an architectural recess.

The revolution which Lysippos' art signified in its new grasp of the human body (see pages 214–17) is expressed not only by the figure of the standing athlete, but also in the seated or in the relaxed supported posture. This *Hermes,* whose youthful elasticity corresponds to the new Lysippian ideals, introduced into sculpture the motif of a foot resting on a support. The messenger of the gods, pausing to lace his sandals, has been interrupted. He turns his head, as though he has heard the voice of Zeus giving him new orders.

Hermes. Copy of a bronze original by Lysippos (?). Marble, height 60⅝". c. 320 B.C. Ny Carlsberg Glyptotek, Copenhagen

Wrestler. Copy of an original of c. 330 B.C. Marble, height with base 76³/₄". Staatliche Kunstsammlungen, Dresden

This figure of an athlete, created under the influence of Lysippos, probably shows a wrestler tensed to begin a contest with an opponent who is not shown.

The alert preparedness of the young man, who turns his head as though toward a new threat, has something in common with the violent energy of Aristonautes (see page 220).

Nike (Winged Victory of Samothrace). ▶ Marble, height 96¹/₂" (originally 113³/₈"). c. 200 B.C. From Samothrace. The Louvre, Paris

The *Nike* of Samothrace harks back to an older theme which Paionios (see page 172) had been the first to ▶ represent in a completely novel way with his *Nike* in Olympia. His goddess of victory floats down from Olympus as a divine being, while this one stands on the very real prow of a ship to which she has brought triumph.

The specific victory at sea glorified in this monument cannot be positively identified. A similar Nike, standing on a ship and blowing a trumpet, appears on a coin of Demetrios Poliorketes which celebrated his defeat of Ptolemy at sea in 306 B.C. However, the later discovery of a hand of the *Nike* of Samothrace (fragments of which are in Vienna) show that it was held out, empty, in front of her.

The divine vision of Nike, her garments wet with sea spray whipped about by the wind, appears as a fellow combatant leading her followers to victory.

Philosopher. Roman copy of an original painting of the mid-third century B.C. Height 63″. Wall painting (detail) from the great hall of the House of P. Fannius Synistor, near Boscoreale. Museo Nazionale, Naples

In the empire of Alexander, the figure of the philosopher approached that of the ruler in importance, just as Aristotle, Alexander's tutor, had brought about an unprecedented fusion of power and intellect. As the complementary extremes of human existence, these qualities shaped a world that was also outwardly transformed. The philosopher, leaning on his staff and thoughtfully gazing toward the royal figures from whom he is separated by a painted column (see page 246), is probably the moving force behind the event illustrated. The column, which forms part of the over-all decoration, also has the effect of setting the philosopher apart, of giving him the appearance of an outsider who is not really present at the proceedings.

Funerary monument of a youth. Marble, height 66⅛″. c. 330–320 ▶ B.C. From the Ilissos, Athens. National Museum, Athens

The tombstone from the Ilissos (facing page) depicts figures from two different worlds: the youth is dead and his father has survived him. Nothing in the external appearance of the figures specifically states this, yet the artist leaves no doubt in our minds. The pensiveness of the old man as he gazes on the splendid figure of his son leads the observer to meditate on the transitoriness of what on earth seemed almost perfect. The young hunter, whose attendant and dog grieve at being abandoned, seems to fix admonishing eyes on the passer-by. The relief, which had an architectural frame (see page 220), far surpasses the general run of grave reliefs. Demetrios of Phaleron's decree (between 317 and 307 B.C.) against funerary luxury brought these to a sudden end.

Tomb relief of a young woman. Marble, height 68⁷/₈″. c. 330–320 B.C. From Rhamnous (Attica). National Museum, Athens

Although his pose is in many ways similar to that of the dead youth on the Ilissos tombstone (see page 225), the man shown here is the survivor, who gazes sadly at his dead wife. He gives her his hand in farewell, while she turns away with an eloquent gesture of her left arm, seemingly impelled by an inexorable force to continue her journey to the realm of the dead. The "ethos" of this work is reminiscent of the early fifth century B.C. (see pages 131, 133, 141).

The sentimentality of funerary reliefs (see page 202), as well as the markedly feminine note in art, have disappeared. How the new masculine ideal reinstated by Alexander also influenced the treatment of the female figure is clearly evident here.

Medea Meditating the Murder of Her Children. Copy of an original painting by Timomachos (?). Fragment of a wall painting, height 53⁷/₈″. Original c. 280 B.C. From Herculaneum. Museo Nazionale, Naples

This surviving fragment of a larger painting shows Medea, sword in hand, wrestling with the decision whether or not to murder her children. The actual presence of the children is quite unnecessary for an understanding of the situation. Posterity marveled at the brilliant psychological representation of inner conflict in the *Medea* of Timomachos.

"When the hand of Timomachos drew Medea, cursed and torn between her children and the fury that raged within her, it took the greatest pains to capture her inner conflict—her inclination to pity as well as her tendency to madness. It succeeded in both" (Antiphilos, *Anth. Pal.,* 4, 136). Pliny (35, 36) reports that Caesar paid eighty talents (about $250,000) for this painting.

227

Aphrodite. Marble, height 80¹/₄″. Second century B.C. From Melos. The Louvre, Paris

The "*Venus de Milo*" was discovered on the island of Melos, together with the signature of a certain Alexandros of Antioch on the Maeander, who would appear to have been the sculptor. Here the artist has successfully adapted a fourth-century model. In her left hand the goddess probably held an apple, symbol of the island, whereas the prototype had held a shield in both hands, in which she looked at her reflection. The loss of the arms shows off to best advantage the elegant spiral twist of the body which has made this one of the best-known works of Antiquity. This sturdy feminine ideal is in sharp contrast to that of the fourth century B.C.

Zeus and Hera. Copy of an original painting of c. 300 B.C. Wall painting, height 50⁸/₄″. From the House of the Tragic Poet, Pompeii. Museo Nazionale, Naples

The Pompeian artist who made this picture into a companion piece to the Briseis painting (see page 209) probably saw a relationship between the two scenes; or perhaps his only reason for doing so was to have both Briseis and Hera look directly out of the painting at the observer.

The scene represented is not the well-known meeting of Zeus and Hera on Mount Ida, so important for the Trojan War (Homer, *Iliad*, XIV), but rather the sacred marriage of the two divinities. Like a shy bride, Hera is ushered in by a winged figure. Symbols of Cybele on the central pillar are a reference to Asia Minor, but the boys at the lower right have not yet been identified. The relationship of this picture to the Briseis painting is, in fact, only superficial; for the pitifully pleading expression of Briseis produces a different mood from that invoked by the self-consciously thoughtful gaze of Hera, who stands beside Zeus as his equal. Historically, the picture undoubtedly symbolizes the union of Asia Minor with Greece.

Apotheosis of Homer. Detail of a relief by Archelaos of Priene, after an original painting. Marble, over-all height 45¹/₄″; height of the frieze 12⁵/₈″. Original c. 220–200 B.C. From Bovillae (Marino, near Rome). British Museum, London

In the upper portion of this votive relief of a poet, Archelaos of Priene depicted the Muses according to a well-known statuary prototype. In the bottom register, Homer is honored by Myth, History, Poetry, Tragedy, Comedy, Nature, Virtue, Faithfulness, and Wisdom. Inscriptions explain the personifications. Behind Homer stands a royal couple, probably Ptolemy IV Philopator (221–204 B.C.) and Arsinoë III, who had erected a temple to Homer in Alexandria. This may have been the site of the original painting.

The particular honor in which Homer was held in the third century B.C., resulting in an intensive scientific-philological study of the *Iliad* and the *Odyssey,* can be explained by the importance that this period set on his heroes as examples. The heroic ideal, given new currency by Alexander, was Achilles, whose tomb near Troy the Macedonian king had visited.

Late Greek art not only created one of the most impressive portraits of Homer, but also expressed in paintings its high esteem of the poet. The center of the cult was the Homereion in Alexandria, the scholarship of which is reflected in the allegorical figures surrounding Homer in this relief (facing page). Indications that the *Iliad* and the *Odyssey* were also illustrated are provided by accounts of mosaics with series of pictures from Homer, and by the "Homeric cups"—terra-cotta bowls with scenes from the Homeric epics, which are probably cheap copies of expensive gold or silver cups.

Isis Receiving Io in Egypt. Copy of an original of the third century B.C. Height 55$^1/_8$″. Wall painting from the temple of Isis in Pompeii. Museo Nazionale, Naples

In her flight, Io, who was loved by Zeus and transformed into a cow by the jealous Hera (see page 205), finally reached Egypt, where she was warmly received. This myth enabled the painter to allude to the old bonds between Greece and Egypt, which were renewed during the Ptolemaic period. Presumably the original was in Alexandria, which was a center of poetry and learning in the third century B.C.

In its heroic-solemn mood, as well as in the fact that both seem to point toward the future, the *Io* picture is related to the *Hera* painting (see page 229). The promise of prosperity, which the renewal of former bonds will promote, is the common idea upon which both paintings are based.

Several kings of Egypt and Pergamon were surnamed "Philometor" (He Who Honors His Mother). The brothers Eumenes II (197–159 B.C.) and Attalos II (159–138 B.C.) honored their mother Apollonis by erecting a temple in Kyzikos. Here were depicted legendary examples of the love between mother and child: two brothers, Amphion and Zethos, revenge the ill treatment which their mother Antiope had suffered at the hand of Dirke by tying the latter to the horns of a wild bull. The learning that sought inspiration in the past found here a theme in which active expression could be given to that respect which determined the relationship of the kings to their mother.

The original painting was also copied in Pompeii and was probably the model for the gigantic marble *Farnese Bull* in Naples.

Stag Hunt. Pebble mosaic by Gnosis, height 9′ 10″. c. 310 B.C. At Pella (Macedonia)

◄ *The Punishment of Dirke,* after an original painting of the second century B.C. Translucent green quartz (prase), c. 1 × 1″. c. 30 B.C. From Aquileia (Italy). Museo Nazionale, Aquileia

The hunts which Alexander staged in the "paradises," the hunting reserves of the Persian kings, gave new life to the ancient ideal of pitting the strength of man against that of wild beasts (see page 34). A sculptural group by Leochares and Lysippos depicted the fight with the lion in which Alexander almost lost his life. A hunting scene was also included in the series of Alexander paintings (see pages 211, 212). This stag hunt signed by Gnosis was the central panel of a mosaic floor. It is framed by rich scrollwork with a wave-pattern border. This and other mosaics from Pella reveal the influence of the great painters of Alexander's time.

The Gauls, who had invaded Asia Minor, were defeated by Attalos I (241–197 B.C.) at the source of the Kaikos (modern Bakir). The victory was glorified in a large monument on the citadel of Pergamon. The monument was centered on the statue of a Gaul who, in the face of inevitable defeat, has killed his wife and is in the act of committing suicide. Fragments of the pedestal were also found, as well as the signature of the famous artist Epigonos. The group in the Terme Museum is a copy made in Asia Minor that may have been intended for Rome originally. In Italy, the Gauls were decisively beaten in 222 B.C., after they had harassed Rome for over a century. Attalos I, an ally of the Romans, may have taken this opportunity to underscore their mutual interests through such a gift.

Boy Wrestling with a Goose. Copy of a bronze original by Boethos. Marble, height 33¹/₈″. Late third century B.C. Glyptothek, Munich

In its formal allusion to heroic groups, this childish play seems to point to future heroic deeds. The little boy is not just any boy. Despite his physical exertions, his carefully arranged curls remain in place. Pliny (34, 84) gives the work as that of Boethos, who was even more renowned as a silversmith. The goose in the bronze original may well have been plated with silver.

An interest in the natural sciences, and particularly the romantic concept of nature as the fount of life, make a landscape seem worthy of representation. Not since Cretan times had nature played such an important part in art as it did in the third century B.C. It is, however, a nature in which the transforming hand of man is evident. The artist draws it into his life as a divine power which he honors and cherishes; and these landscapes therefore usually have a sacred character. The scene above seems to have inspired the poet who wrote:

> Icy waters cascading from the broken rock, rejoice!
> And shepherd-whittled figures of the nymphs;
> Basins of the spring and these thousand images of you, O virgins,
> Soaked in its waters, rejoice you also!

> LEONIDAS OF TARENTUM, *Anth. Gr.*, IX, 326
> (third century B.C.)

Drinking Doves. Copy of a mosaic by Sosos of the second century B.C. $33^1/_2 \times 38^5/_8''$. From Hadrian's Villa, near Tivoli. Capitoline Museum, Rome

Four doves have settled on the rim of a metal basin filled with water, where they look around, preen themselves, and drink. They are tame birds, and a scene like this could only take place in a wealthy house where costly vessels stood in the open. The gulf between nature and culture has been successfully bridged, just as it has in the painting of the spring in the rocks (see facing page).

Three Roman mosaics, including this one, correspond in theme to a mosaic by Sosos of Pergamon which depicted doves perched on the edge of a wine cup. Pliny (36, 184) was particularly impressed by the fact that the shadow of the drinking bird was cast on the surface of the water. Our example is an exceptionally fine copy and was originally the centerpiece (emblema) of a large floor mosaic.

The Finding of Telephos (detail). Copy of a Pergamene original of shortly after 190 B.C. Height of the detail $25^5/_8$". Wall painting from the "basilica" in Herculaneum. Museo Nazionale, Naples

The idyllic group of the doe suckling Telephos, son of Herakles, comprises the lower left corner of a painting which depicts Herakles' discovery of Telephos in Arcadia. At the same time, it represents the greatness of the Pergamene kingdom, which reached the height of power under Eumenes II (197–159 B.C.) and of which Telephos was the mythical founder (see pages 250, 252).

"The intercrossing of the limbs of a delicate nursing boy with the nimble animal form of a graceful hind is a composition of such artistry that it surpasses all admiration" (Goethe).

Boy Pulling a Thorn from His Foot. Copy of an original of the third century B.C. Bronze, height 28³/₄". Palazzo dei Conservatori, Rome

The *Spinario* ("Thorn Puller") is known to have been in Rome since at least the twelfth century, from which time onward it has been used as a basis for all kinds of variations on the theme. Even in Antiquity there was no lack of grotesque thorn pullers, in which the original idea had been transformed into something coarse and ridiculous. The Capitoline figure reproduces the original, in which an insignificant act is used to portray the beauty of the youthful body. He is a well-bred boy, nicely groomed, whose tender foot has been injured; and this trivial incident shows the painful discovery of the alienation of the cultivated man from raw nature—a nature which he seeks out, all the same. The significance of this piece would be lost if the boy were a mere peasant lad.

◀ *Veiled Head.* Painted terra cotta, height ³/₄″. Third century B.C. From Cyprus. British Museum, London

This head of a woman, whose face is partially hidden by a veil, was part of a Tanagra figurine, perhaps of a dancer. The way in which the flimsy material covers yet reveals the lips and chin has been masterfully rendered. Terra-cotta figurines from Tanagra (Boeotia) were popular throughout the Greek world (see also page 244).

Aphrodite bends over her small son, who is sitting on a rock, and holds him fast with both hands. She seems to be giving him a lesson in archery, or perhaps she is aiming his arrow at a specific target.

The satyrs—originally wild creatures in Dionysos' retinue, half man and half beast—were completely humanized and seen in an ideal light in the fourth century B.C., particularly by Praxiteles (see page 185). Now, once more, they regain something of their original coarseness.

This frequently copied group of a satyr seeking to embrace a lovely nymph, who offers a rather ineffective resistance, embodies the carefree, joyous essence of nature's creatures as the antithesis of the harrowed and thoughtful life of reality (see also page 243). The sculpture has very little depth and its outlines are more or less confined to a square; yet the composition offers a new aspect from every angle and suffers in no way from a feeling of restriction.

Aphrodite and Eros. Gold ring, ⁷/₈ × ³/₄″. Third century B.C. From Kalymnos (island between Samos and Rhodes). State Museums, Berlin

◀ *Nymph and Satyr.* Copy of an original of the late third century B.C. Marble, 23⁵/₈″. From Trastevere, Rome. Palazzo dei Conservatori, Rome

Sleeping Satyr. Original or copy of a work of the late ▶ *Sleeping Satyr*. Original or copy of a work of the late third century B.C. Marble, height 84⁵/₈″. Restorations on the rock are by Bernini (1598–1680), on the body by Pacetti (1758–1826). From the vicinity of Castel Sant'Angelo, Rome. Glyptothek, Munich

The so-called *Barberini Faun* (facing page) shows a drunken satyr (see page 240), sunk in sleep on a rock, the very picture of absolute unconcern and unity with nature. At the same time, he is a symbol of that inexhaustible source of strength from which mankind continuously renews itself. In Antiquity, water bubbled from a hole in the rock.

Old Peasant Woman. Copy of an original of c. 200 B.C. Marble, height 49⁵/₈″. From the Via della Consolazione, Rome. The Metropolitan Museum of Art, New York

This peasant woman holds two chickens and a basket of fruit in her left hand. Her extended right hand probably offered other wares for sale. A genre picture such as this shows that the sensitivity of Late Greek art for down-to-earth subjects was not restricted to poetry. Once again, the rustic theme, closely bound to nature, contains within it an element of contrast: the woman from the country is going to the city to sell her wares.

The outspoken realism evident in this figure of an old woman is characteristic of this phase of Greek art. The love of detail is in conformity with an attitude of mind that sees the great in the small and recognizes detail as an essential part of the whole. This naturalism is an integral part of the work of art taken in its entirety.

Two Women Gossiping. Painted terra cotta, height 7$^{1}/_{8}$″. Second century B.C. From Myrina (Asia Minor). British Museum, London

Terra-cotta figurines, originally votive or tomb offerings, seem to have partially lost this characteristic as early as the fourth century B.C. and were used as decorative objects in Late Greek times. In the modest dimensions and humble material of these figures, art began to take an interest in the wholly private side of life. Their intimacy endows these miniature works of art with a special charm and makes them easier to understand than the more important monumental sculpture. The two women are shown seated on a couch and leaning toward each other, the older one with some reserve. The younger girl, on the left, shows greater interest; presumably she is receiving some fascinating piece of information from her older friend.

Royal Couple. Cameo of Indian sardonyx with nine alternating brown and white layers, height $4^1/_2''$, width $11^1/_4''$. The portion with the strange collar is restored. First half of third century B.C. Kunsthistorisches Museum, Vienna

Works of art in semiprecious stone now became more important than ever. Whole vessels were carved out of expensive stones which had previously been used only for seals. Particularly popular were cameos with the image of the ruler, a few examples of which have survived through having belonged to Roman emperors and then passed into the possession of the church. Identification of this ruler with his richly decorated helmet and of the woman with an ornamented diadem is still uncertain, but they are probably Ptolemies—perhaps Ptolemy II and Arsinoë II. Such portrait cameos were made for, or on the orders of, the rulers and were presented as honorary awards or gifts.

Macedonian King and Seated Woman. Roman copy (c. 40 B.C.) of an original painting of the mid-third century B.C. Height 63″. Wall painting (detail) from the great hall of the House of P. Fannius Synistor, near Boscoreale. Museo Nazionale, Naples

The peaceful association of the two figures, the prophetic look of the woman sitting on the floor, and the intensity with which the man in the background fixes her lend a haunting air to the picture. Some say it depicts a visit to the underworld; but a more precise interpretation is hampered by the fact that the right-hand third of the picture is missing. The man in the left in this detail can be identified by his cap and shield as a Macedonian king. Further to the left, separated by a column, stands the thoughtful philosopher (see page 224), who seems to be the spiritual force behind the scene represented.

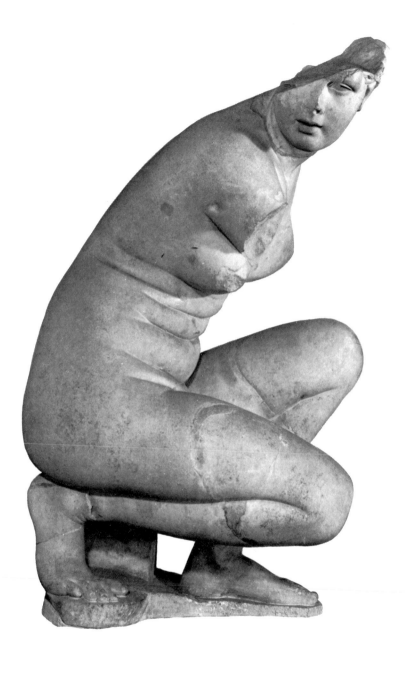

Crouching Aphrodite. Copy of the original by Doidalsas of Bithynia. Marble, height 40¹/₈″. Mid-third century B.C. From Hadrian's Villa at Tivoli. Terme Museum, Rome

Of all Aphrodite statues, this is perhaps the most intimate. The goddess, unaware that she is observed, crouches down to her bath with the naturalness of a nymph. She seems to have turned her head in response to a noise which has broken the silence of her solitude. This motif, originated by Doidalsas, was later reproduced in many variations.

Athena. Marble, height (with base) 11′ 6¼″, (without base) 10′ 2″. Second century B.C. From the Library of Pergamon. State Museums, Berlin

This statue of Athena stood in the Library of Pergamon, second in fame to that of Alexandria, as the patroness of learning. She was modeled on the *Athena Parthenos* of Pheidias (see page 153), but is not an exact copy of that masterpiece. Such a return to the forms of Pheidias' cult image is not a sign of artistic decadence, but an expression of the indebtedness of the time to the merits of the Greek past. Furthermore, she was made for display in an art museum in which important works were on show. Under Athena's patronage, Pergamon intended to pursue her ancient cultural heritage, and even to vie with Athens in this respect.

Scenes of frightening brutality are fairly frequent in Greek ▶ art, and the battle of the gods and giants is waged mercilessly. Here, the constellation Engonasin, fighting on the side of the Olympians, is lifted into the air by a serpent-footed giant, who bites him in the arm. His victory is by no means certain.

The compensating beauty with which the art of the fourth century B.C. had covered the horrors of battle (see pages 179, 212) is to be sought in vain in this gigantomachy. Some artists of the fifth century B.C., however, had depicted centauromachies (see pages 134, 152, 165) with the same horrific reality.

Head of a Giant. From the north frieze of the Great Altar of Pergamon. Marble, c. 180 B.C. State Museums, Berlin

The Great Altar of Zeus and Athena in Pergamon was probably erected by Eumenes II (197–159 B.C.), although the few surviving letters of the dedicatory inscription could also be restored to read Attalos [I] (241–197 B.C.). The frieze, some four hundred feet long, is the most imposing relief in the whole of Greek art. The creator of the altar building is assumed to have been Menekrates, whom Ausonius (*Mosella*, 307) names together with six other builders of victory monuments. Menekrates also appears among the names of sculptors that have been preserved, but these seem only to be artisans who executed the slabs after a master plan. Other names of artists are Dionysiades, Orestes, and Theorretos. The names of the gods and giants were also chiseled in the marble, making it easier to understand the representational program of the relief, which must otherwise have been difficult to decipher even for a cultured individual. The gigantomachy undoubtedly reflects the battle of the Pergamenes with the Gauls, interpreted as the victory of culture over nonculture. In just the same way, in the early fifth century B.C., had the Athenians represented their victory over the Persians in the guise of battles with centaurs and Amazons.

Their own mythical past was the theme of the smaller frieze in the raised altar court. The story of Telephos, son of Herakles and Auge (see page 238), who as the first king of Mysia was the forefather of the Pergamene kings, is narrated in a series of consecutive scenes. Abandoned by his mother in the wilderness, Telephos was nourished by a wild animal, like Romulus and Remus, the founders of Rome, a city with which the Pergamene kings early entered into good relations; and it was Rome that eventually inherited their kingdom (133 B.C.).

Leto and Apollo. From the east frieze of the Great Altar of Pergamon. Marble, height 90^1/$_2$″. c. 180 B.C. State Museums, Berlin

Zeus Hurling His Thunderbolt against Porphyrion. From the east frieze of the Great Altar of Pergamon. Marble, height 90¹/₂″. c. 180 B.C. State Museums, Berlin

The place of honor in the middle of the east side was given to Zeus and Athena, who are shown fighting side by side. The thunderbolt of Zeus has already pierced the thigh of a giant, and the god launches a second bolt at Porphyrion, a serpent-footed giant who attempts to shield himself with a lion's skin. Zeus's eagle also takes part in the battle. A wounded giant is on his knees between these two adversaries.

The surging, powerful movement that enlivens the basically monotonous battle scenes is developed in a relatively contained relief. However, the outlines are softened by rear views, overlapping of the figures, and (originally) by painting, and the figures are free and unconstrained in their movements. As in classic relief, they completely fill the height of the frieze.

◄ Apollo as an archer—similar to the *Apollo Belvedere* (see page 218)—stands over the fallen giant Ephialtes, while Leto thrusts her burning torch into the face of the winged Tityos (?) lying on the ground.

This scene of the finding of Telephos is strongly reminiscent of the painting of the same subject (see page 238), although here it is a lioness that suckles the child. This deviation from the literary version of the myth which was followed in the painting is an obvious allusion to the boy's royal future.

The Telephos frieze of the altar is much more picturesque than the Great Frieze, since the figures are set in a landscape and space is left free above their heads. The two friezes must be contemporary, the differences in style being explained by the diversity of their themes. Parts of the Telephos frieze remained unfinished.

The Finding of Telephos. Detail of the Telephos frieze of the Great Altar of Pergamon. Marble, height of the frieze, $62^{1}/_{4}''$; of the fragment $42^{1}/_{2}''$. c. 180 B.C. State Museums, Berlin

Chronological Tables: I. Summary

B.C.		
2500	Early Helladic culture	Early Minoan culture
2400		
2300		
2200		
2100		
2000		
1900		Middle Minoan culture
1800	Middle Helladic culture	
1700		
1600		
1500	Late Helladic culture	Late Minoan culture
1400		Crete comes under Mycenaean rule
1300		
1200		Trojan War
1100	Doric migrations	
1000	Protogeometric art	
900	Early Geometric art / Severe Geometric art	
800	Mature Geometric art / Late Geometric art	Development of Greek alphabetic script / Homer
700		
600	Archaic art	
500	Classical art	510/508 Democracy established in Athens
400	Late classical art	
300	Late Greek art of Alexander's empire	336–323 Alexander the Great
200		168 Battle of Pydna / 146 Destruction of Corinth

II. Greek Art, Culture, and History

B.C. 1100	Sub-Mycenaean art	Doric migrations Collapse of the 　　Mycenaean empire	Mycenaean syllabic script 　　disappears
11th C.		Athens remains in the hands 　　of the Ionians	
	Protogeometric art		
1000			

1000	Protogeometric art	Formation of the 　　Greek city-states	Creation of legends 　　of Mycenaean rulers 　　and the Trojan War
10th C.			
900			

900	Early Geometric art		
9th C.	Severe Geometric art		
800			

800	Mature Geometric art Ivory and bronze statuettes		Development of Greek 　　alphabetic script
		776 First list of winners 　　in the Olympian games	
8th C.		754 Establishment of Spartan 　　ephorate	
	Late Geometric art	740–720 First Messenian War	Homer, *Iliad* and *Odyssey*
700			

700	Early Archaic art *Sphyrelaton* figures Proto-Corinthian vases Early Attic vases		Hesiod of Askra, *Theogony* 　　and *Works and Days* Archilochos of Paros
7th C.		660–640 Second Messenian War	Tyrtaios in Sparta Alkman in Sparta
	Mature Archaic art Kouroi Corinthian vases	627–585 Periander, 　　Tyrant of Corinth	
600	Nessos amphora (Athens)	Draco's reforms in Athens	

	Art	Events	Literature / Philosophy

600
 	
6th C.
 	
500
	Standing Goddess of Berlin
	Calf Bearer
	Temple of Apollo, Corinth
	Peplos Kore
	
	Exekias
	Late Archaic art
	Korai
	Kimon of Kleonai
	Red-figure vase painting
		594 Solon's reforms in Athens
		
		560–527 Peisistratos,
		    Tyrant of Athens
		
		538–522 Polykrates, Tyrant of Samos
		528–510 Hippias, Tyrant of Athens
		514 Assassination of Hipparchos
		    by Harmodios and Aristogeiton
		510/508 Democracy established
		    in Athens by Kleisthenes
			Sappho, Alkaios
			610–c. 546 Anaximandros
			585 Thales predicts
			    eclipse of the sun
			c. 570–c. 485 Anakreon
			c. 570 Birth of Theognis
			565 Founding of the
			    Panathenaic festival
			
			534 Thespis wins prize at Athens

500 5th C. 400	Temple of Aphaia, Aegina Classical art Temple of Zeus, Olympia *Poseidon* from Cape Artemision 448–432 Parthenon Myron, Pheidias, Polykleitos, Kresilas 437–432 Propylaia Temple of Apollo, Bassae Paionios Erechtheion Temple of Athena Nike Zeuxis, Meidias	500–494 Ionian uprising 490 Battle of Marathon 480 Battle of Salamis 479 Battle of Plataia 478/477 Formation of Delian League 449 Peace of Kallias 443–429 Perikles 431–404 Peloponnesian War 421–415 Peace of Nikias 415–413 Sicilian expedition 404 Defeat of Athens 404–403 Rule of the Thirty	c. 544–c. 484 Herakleitos 525–456 Aischylos 518–438 Pindar c. 513 Birth of Parmenides c. 496–406 Sophokles c. 485–c. 425 Herodotos c. 485–c. 406 Euripides 469–399 Sokrates c. 460–c. 400 Thucydides c. 460–c. 370 Demokritos c. 450–c. 385 Aristophanes

400
 	
4th C.
 	
300
	Late classical art
	Grave stele of Dexileos, Timotheos
	Tholos in Delphi
	Temple of Asklepios, Epidauros
	Kerch vases
	Praxiteles
	Mausoleum of Halikarnassos
	    Nikias, Skopas, Bryaxis
	334 Choragic monument of Lysikrates
	Late Greek art, Lysippos
	Leochares, *Battle of Alexander*
	Apelles, Pella mosaics
		400–386 War between Athens and Sparta
		395–386 Corinthian War
		386 Peace of Antilkidas
		379 Pelopidas in Thebes
		378–372 Formation of second Athenian
		    maritime league
		371 Battle of Leuktra
		362 Epaminondas killed at Mantineia
		359–336 Philip II of Macedon
		338 Battle of Chaironeia
		336–323 Alexander the Great
		323–281 Wars of the Diadochi
		301 Battle of Ipsos
			436–338 Isokrates
			c. 430–c. 354 Xenophon
			c. 429–347 Plato
			384–322 Aristotle
			384–322 Demosthenes
			c. 370–c. 287 Theophrastos
			c. 342–c. 292 Menander
			c. 341–270 Epikouros
			335–263 Zeno

300
 	
3rd C.
 	
200
	Followers of Lysippos
	    and Leochares
	Boethos
	Doidalsas
	
	Spinario
	
	Statues of Gauls
	
	Barberini Faun
		295–285 Demetrios Poliorketes in Athens
		283 Philetairos founds
		    Kingdom of Pergamon
		280–220 Period of the Epigonoi
		279 Gauls in Delphi
		276 Antiochos I defeats Gallic invaders
		263–241 Eumenes I of Pergamon
		Attalos I of Pergamon (241–197)
		    defeats the Gauls
		223–187 Antiochos III (the Great)
		221–203 Ptolemy IV
		220 Beginning of the decline
			c. 305–c. 240 Kallimachos
			c. 280 Zenodotos of Ephesos
			    edits Homer's *Iliad* and
			    Odyssey in Alexandria
			c. 280–207 Chrysippos
			c. 275–194 Eratosthenes
			
			Homereion in Alexandria

200
 	
2nd C.
 	
100
	Nike of Samothrace
	
	The Finding of Telephos
	Great Altar of Pergamon
	Myrina terra cottas
	
	Aphrodite of Melos
		200–197 Second Macedonian War
		197–159 Eumenes II of Pergamon
		171–168 Third Macedonian War
		168 Roman victory at Pydna
		159–138 Attalos II of Pergamon
		146 Mummius destroys Corinth
		138–133 Attalos III of Pergamon
		133 Pergamon bequeathed
		    to the Romans
			c. 185–109 Panaitios
			168 Polybius deported to Rome
			156 Karneades leads Athenian
			    delegation of philosophers
			    to Rome

Pella

Dherveni

Thasos

Corfu

Cape Artemision

Thermon

Amphissa

Delphi

Orchomenos

Chalkis

Eretria

Thebes

Tanagra

Athens

Megara

Piraeus

Corinth

Aegina

Mycenae

Mideia

Epidauros

Argos

Tiryns

Sounion

Olympia

Bassae

Lerna

Tegea

Sparta

Pylos

Vaphio

Siphnos

Melos

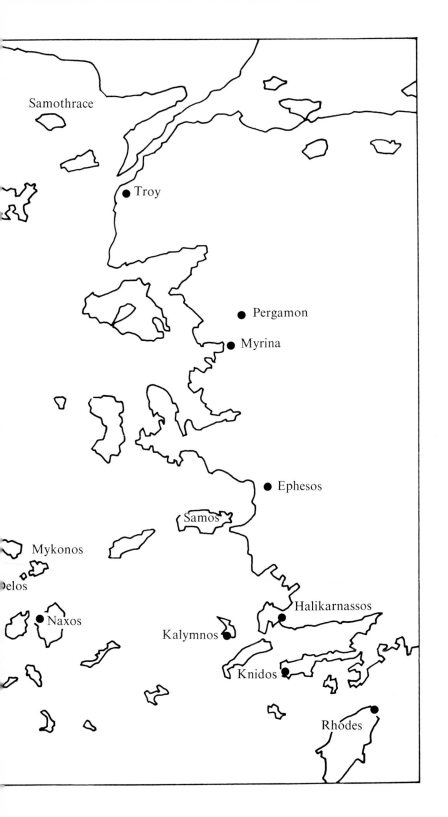

Samothrace

● Troy

● Pergamon

● Myrina

● Ephesos

Samos

Mykonos

Delos

● Naxos

Kalymnos ●

Halikarnassos ●

Knidos ●

Rhodes ●

The Greek World

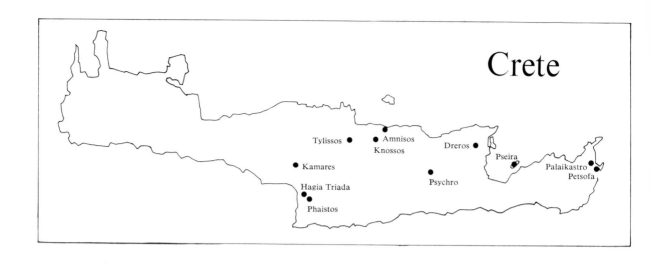

Crete

Tylissos
Amnisos
Knossos
Dreros
Pseira
Kamares
Palaikastro
Petsofa
Psychro
Hagia Triada
Phaistos

Bibliography

GENERAL WORKS

ARIAS, P. E., and HIRMER, M., *A History of 1000 Years of Greek Vase Painting,* New York, 1963

BECATTI, G., *Scultura greca,* Milan, 1961, 2 vols.

BOARDMAN, J., et al., *Greek Art and Architecture,* New York, 1967

COOK, R. M., *Greek Painted Pottery,* 2nd ed., London, 1966

CURTIUS, L., *Die klassische Kunst Griechenlands,* Potsdam, 1938

DEVAMBEZ, P., *Greek Painting,* New York, 1963

DINSMOOR, W. B., *The Architecture of Ancient Greece,* 3rd ed., London, 1950

HAFNER, G., *Geschichte der griechischen Kunst,* Zurich, 1961

KÄHLER, H., *Das griechische Metopenbild,* Munich, 1949

KÄHLER, H., *Der griechische Tempel: Wesen und Gestalt,* Berlin, 1964

KRAAY, C. M., and HIRMER, M., *Greek Coins,* New York, 1966

KRAIKER, W., *Die Malerei der Griechen,* Stuttgart, 1958

LAWRENCE, A. W., *Greek Architecture,* 2nd ed., Baltimore, 1967

LIPPOLD, G., *Die griechische Plastik,* 5th ed., Munich, 1950

LÜBKE, W., and PERNICE, E., *Die Kunst der Griechen,* 17th ed. completely revised by B. Sarne, Vienna, 1948

LULLIES, R., and HIRMER, M., *Greek Sculpture,* New York, 1960

NEPPI MODONA, A., *Gli edifici teatrali greci e romani,* Florence, 1961

OVERBECK, J., *Die antiken Schriftquellen zur Geschichte der bildenden Künste bei den Griechen,* Leipzig, 1868

PFUHL, E., *Malerei und Zeichnung der Griechen,* Munich, 1923, 3 vols. (Shorter version, translated by J. D. Beazley, *Masterpieces of Greek Drawing and Painting,* New York, 1955)

PICARD, C., *Manuel d'archéologie grecque,* Vols. I–IV, Paris, 1935–63

RICHTER, G. M. A., *A Handbook of Greek Art,* 5th ed., New York, 1967

RICHTER, G. M. A., *The Portraits of the Greeks,* London, 1965, 3 vols.

RICHTER, G. M. A., *The Sculpture and Sculptors of the Greeks,* 3rd ed., New Haven, 1950

RICHTER, G. M. A., *Three Critical Periods in Greek Sculpture,* New York, 1951

ROBERTSON, D. S., *A Handbook of Greek and Roman Architecture,* new ed., New York, 1969

ROBERTSON, M., *Greek Painting,* Cleveland, 1959

SCHUCHHARDT, W. H., *Die Epochen der griechischen Plastik,* Baden-Baden, 1959

SCHUCHHARDT, W. H., *Die Kunst der Griechen,* Berlin, 1940

WEBSTER, T. B. L., *Greek Terracottas,* Edinburgh, 1950

CRETAN-MYCENAEAN ART

BOSSERT, H. T., *The Art of Ancient Crete,* London, 1937
CHADWICK, J., *The Decipherment of Linear B,* New York, 1958
Corpus der minoischen und mykenischen Siegel, Vol. I, Berlin, 1964, and Vol. VIII, Mainz, 1966. In progress
DEMARGNE, P., *The Birth of Greek Art,* Pt. I, New York, 1964
EVANS, A. J., *The Palace of Minos at Knossos,* London, 1921–36, 5 vols.
HUTCHINSON, R. W., *Prehistoric Crete,* Magnolia, Mass., 1965
KARO, G., *Die Schachtgräber von Mykenai,* Munich, 1930–33, 2 vols.
MARINATOS, S., and HIRMER, M., *Crete and Mycenae,* New York, 1960
MATZ, F., *The Art of Crete and Early Greece,* New York, 1965
MATZ, F., *Kreta, Mykene, Troja: Die minoische und die homerische Welt,* Stuttgart, 1956
MYLONAS, G. E., *Ancient Mycenae: The Capital City of Agamemnon,* Princeton, 1966
MYLONAS, G. E., *Mycenae and the Mycenaean Age,* Princeton, 1966
PENDLEBURY, J. D. S., *The Archaeology of Crete,* New York, 1965
SCHACHERMEYR, F., *Die ältesten Kulturen Griechenlands,* Stuttgart, 1955
ZERVOS, C., *L'Art de la Crète néolithique et minoenne,* Paris, 1956

EARLY GREEK ART

DEMARGNE, P., *The Birth of Greek Art,* Pt. II, New York, 1964
DESBOROUGH, V. R. D'A., *Protogeometric Pottery,* New York, 1952
MATZ, F., *Geschichte der griechischen Kunst,* Vol. I, Frankfurt, 1950
OHLY, D., *Griechische Goldbleche des 8. Jahrhunderts v. Chr.,* Berlin, 1953

ARCHAIC ART

BEAZLEY, J. D., *Attic Black-Figure Vase-Painters,* New York, 1956
BEAZLEY, J. D., *Attic Red-Figure Vase-Painters,* 2nd ed., New York, 1963, 3 vols.
BEAZLEY, J. D., *The Development of Attic Black-Figure,* Berkeley, 1951
BUSCHOR, E., *Altsamische Standbilder,* Vols. I–V, Berlin, 1934–61
HOMANN-WEDEKING, E., *Die Anfänge der griechischen Grossplastik,* Berlin, 1950
HOMANN-WEDEKING, E., *The Art of Archaic Greece,* New York, 1968
KÜBLER, K., *Altattische Malerei,* Tübingen, 1949

LANGLOTZ, E., and SCHUCHHARDT, W. H., *Archaische Plastik auf der Akropolis,* Frankfurt, 1940
PAYNE, H., and YOUNG, G. M., *Archaic Marble Sculpture from the Acropolis,* 2nd ed., Chester Springs, Pa., 1950
RICHTER, G. M. A., *The Archaic Gravestones of Attica,* Greenwich, Conn., 1961
RICHTER, G. M. A., *Archaic Greek Art against Its Historical Background,* New York, 1949
RICHTER, G. M. A., and RICHTER, I. A., *Kouroi: Archaic Greek Youths,* 2nd ed., Greenwich, Conn., 1960
SCHRADER, H., et al., *Die archaischen Marmorbildwerke der Akropolis,* Frankfurt, 1939

ART OF THE FIFTH CENTURY B.C.

ARIAS, P. E., *Mirone,* Florence, 1940
ARIAS, P. E., *Pheidias,* Catania, 1944
ARIAS, P. E., *Policleto,* Florence, 1964
BECATTI, G., *Problemi fidiaci,* Milan and Florence, 1951
BIANCHI BANDINELLI, R., *Policleto,* Florence, 1938
BROMMER, F., *Die Metopen des Parthenon,* Mainz, 1967
BROMMER, F., *Die Skulpturen der Parthenon-Giebel,* Mainz, 1963
BRUNNSAKER, S., *The Tyrant-Slayers of Kritios and Nesiotes,* Lund, 1955
BUNDGAARD, J. A., *Mnesikles: A Greek Architect at Work,* Copenhagen, 1957
CARPENTER, R., *The Sculpture of the Nike Temple Parapet,* Cambridge, Mass., 1929
DIEPOLDER, H., *Die attischen Grabreliefs des 5. und 4. Jahrhunderts v. Chr.,* Berlin, 1931
JOHANSEN, K. F., *The Attic Grave-Reliefs of the Classical Period,* Copenhagen, 1951
PICKARD-CAMBRIDGE, A. W., *The Theatre of Dionysus in Athens,* New York, 1946
RODENWALDT, G., and HEGE, W., *The Acropolis,* Norman, Okla., 1958
RODENWALDT, G., and HEGE, W., *Olympia,* London, 1936
SCHEFOLD, K., *The Art of Classical Greece,* New York, 1966

ART OF THE FOURTH CENTURY B.C.

ARIAS, P. E., *Skopas,* Rome, 1952
BLINKENBERG, C., *Knidia: Beiträge zur Kenntnis der Praxitelischen Aphrodite,* Copenhagen, 1933
CROME, J. F., *Die Skulpturen des Asklepiostempels von Epidauros,* Berlin, 1951
DOHRN, T., *Attische Plastik vom Tode des Phidias bis zum Wirken der grossen Meister des 4. Jahrhunderts v. Chr.,* Krefeld, 1957
GERKAN, A. VON, and MÜLLER-WIENER, W., *Das Theater von Epidauros,* Stuttgart, 1961
RIZZO, G. E., *Prassitele,* Milan, 1932
ZÜCHNER, W., *Griechische Klappspiegel,* Berlin, 1942

ART OF THE TIME OF ALEXANDER
AND THE DIADOCHI

BIEBER, M., *The Sculpture of the Hellenistic Age,* 2nd ed., New York, 1961

CHARBONNEAUX, J., *La Vénus de Milos,* Bremen, 1958

DOHRN, T., *Die Tyche von Antiochia,* Berlin, 1960

KÄHLER, H., *Der grosse Fries von Pergamon,* Berlin, 1948

LAWRENCE, A. W., *Later Greek Sculpture and Its Influence on East and West,* New York, 1927

LULLIES, R., *Die kauernde Aphrodite,* Munich, 1954

SCHMIDT, E., *The Great Altar of Pergamon,* Leipzig, 1962

SCHOBER, A., *Die Kunst von Pergamon,* Vienna, 1951

WEBSTER, T. B. L., *The Art of Greece: The Age of Hellenism,* New York, 1966

Index

Photo credits: C. Albiker, Ettlingen, p. 40. Alinari, Florence, p. 234. E. Böhm, Mainz, p. 59. Photo Bulloz, Paris, p. 223. Deutsches Archäologisches Institut, Athens, p. 64, 88, 104, 131, 133, 225. G. Hafner, Mainz, p. 14, 15, 32, 34, 38, 42, 45, 46, 47, 50, 51, 54, 56, 57, 58 (2×), 60, 61, 62, 65 upper, 66, 67 (2×), 70, 74, 75, 76, 77, 79, 81, 89, 90, 91, 95, 96, 98, 106, 108, 110, 119, 121, 123, 126, 128, 129, 132, 136, (2×), 143, 144, 145, 146, 147, 149, 153, 155, 158, 159, 160, 161, 162, 163, 165, 168 right, 169, 170, 172, 173, 174, 175, 178, 180, 182, 183, 184, 185, 186, 188, 189, 190, 191, 196, 197, 198, 199, 202, 205, 214, 215, 216, 217, 218, 219, 220, 221, 222, 226, 228, 230, 232, 235, 239, 240, 242, 243, 247, 248, 249, 250, 251. Hirmer Verlag, Munich, p. 13, 18, 19, 36, 39, 44, 48, 97, 150, 152. Holle Verlag, Baden-Baden, p. 16, 22, 24, 25, 27, 28, 29, 30, 33, 37, 53, 55, 71, 78, 85, 103, 116, 122, 137, 187, 224, 236, 237, 244, 252. Internationales Bildarchiv Horst von Irmer, Munich, p. 156, 157, 164, 166. N. Kontos, Athens, p. 35, 49, 63, 105, 109, 114, 115, 117, 120, 142, 167, 179, 181, 207. L. Larsen, Copenhagen, p. 65 lower. J. A. Lavaud, Paris, p. 21, 23, 41. Foto Marburg, Marburg, p. 171. E. Meyer, Vienna, p. 245. C. H. Moessner, Munich, p. 140. J. Remmer, Munich, p. 246. O. Savio, Rome, p. 84. Foto Scala, Florence, p. 93, 118 lower, 127, 141, 154, 168 left, 176, 210–11. M. Seidel, Mittenwald, p. 80, 92, 94, 107, 124, 193, 194, 195, 204, 212, 227, 229, 231. J. Skeel, Ashford, p. 82, 83, 86, 100, 102, 125, 148, 192, 200, 203. Uni-Dia Verlag, Grosshesselohe, nr. Munich, p. 118 upper. T. B. L. Webster, London, p. 40. The author and publisher would like to thank all those who have helped to make possible the produktion of this book.